INDIAN TRIBES
OF NORTH AMERICA

TIGER BOOKS INTERNATIONAL
LONDON

This edition published in 1996 by:
Tiger Books International PLC, Twickenham

This book was designed and produced by
Todtri Productions Limited
P.O. Box 572
New York, NY 10116-0572
Fax: (212) 279-1241

Printed and bound in Singapore

ISBN 1-85501-829-2

Author: Josepha Sherman

Publisher: Robert Tod
Book Designer: Mark Weinberg
Editor: Louise Quale
Picture Research: Ede Rothaus *and* Grace How
Design Assistance: Louise Sullivan

TABLE OF CONTENTS

Foreward..5

The Northwest Coast
and California..6

The Great Plains......................................24

Tribes of the Great
Basin and Plateau...................................64

The Eastern Woodlands
North and South 76

The Southwest 100

Index..142

Appendix..144

4

FOREWORD

For its Native people, America's history begins long before Columbus sailed to the European "New World." Western scholars, maintaining the myth of the New World, believe that a land bridge once joined Siberia and Alaska and that humans travelled over it between 10,000 and 20,000 years ago. One noted scholar argues persuasively that a Paleolithic culture reached America about 100,000 years ago. Dakota history tells them they emerged from the earth six million years ago.

Recently, scholars have discovered evidence that challenges the widespread belief that Native Americans travelled to North America over the Bering Land Bridge. Radiocarbon dating of remains in a rock shelter on a sandstone cliff in northeastern Brazil date to 32,000 years ago. Humans occupied this shelter where charcoal hearths and stone tools were found.

If humans occupied South America, many reason, then perhaps the peoples of North America arrived here from the south, rather than from the north. Thus far we have based most of what we know about pre-Columbian Native peoples on European studies of their eighteenth- and nineteenth-century customs. These studies certainly are marred by European values and beliefs. Rather than starting from the present and working backwards, perhaps we should look at prehistoric cultures and move forward. For example, if we assume that people migrated over the Bering Land Bridge, we need to know who occupied Siberia at that time.

Many Native cultures have more in common with Mediterranean peoples than ancient people from Siberia. What was the influence of pre-Columbian visitors and settlers on America? Evidence shows that Phoenicians, Druids, and Africans visited here nearly 2,000 years ago. On the east coast, many remained and mixed with the American people, thus affecting their culture as well as their language, economy, and physical characteristics.

Finally, we cannot ignore the oral traditions passed on by the elders to the young in everyday life. Much is missing from written accounts of their way of life—both present and past. In the oral tradition, learning is a part of daily life. Children learned about their history, culture, and religious beliefs as a part of their daily activities. They learned several languages in order to trade with other nomadic peoples.

The history of America before Columbus awaits us. Many of the photographs in this book show the American Indian through European eyes. Others celebrate the continuing heritage of Native Americans in modern America. Until we learn more about America before Columbus, Native American life in paintings and photographs speak volumes about their heritage.

Anthony Saenz
President of the Council
for Native American Progress

THE

NORTHWEST COAST

AND CALIFORNIA

THE LAND

Before Europeans settled what is now the Pacific coast of Washington, Oregon, and northern California, the green, wet land was home to several Native American tribes. To the north, indigenous peoples inhabited Alaska, while others to the east made their homes among the snow-capped Cascade Range. This long line of towering, mostly dormant volcanoes runs from Alaska all the way to California, including such well known peaks as Mount Rainier and the still restless Mount St. Helens. To the west, the Pacific Ocean beats against a steep, jagged coastline and a maze of islands. Between the mountains and ocean, the western rain forest— mostly conifers such as fir, spruce, and cedar in Washington and Oregon, and primarily redwoods

Examples of Tsimshian totem poles still stand in Kitwancool, British Columbia.

in northern California—tower above the land. The sadly shrunken remains of that enormous primordial forest now stand only in such protected areas as the Olympic National Forest on Washington's Olympic Peninsula. Before whites settled the area, the forest covered most of the Pacific Northwest in a vast, dense tangle of trees and moss.

To its original inhabitants, the land offered an abundant supply of plant and animal life. Warming ocean currents along the Pacific coastline produced a mild climate, temperate in the summer with relatively gentle winters. Native Americans thanked the Great Mystery for the richness of the land, and many religious rituals focused on the spirits of the sea.

The people told stories of enormous schools of salmon in the rivers, so many that at spawning time a man could walk across their backs from bank to bank without getting his feet wet. In the ocean, crabs, clams, and mussels offered a seemingly endless supply of food, and herring provided food and oil. For those who dared sail on the open sea, whales, seals, and sea lions offered big game hunting.

On land, flocks of ducks, geese, and swans gathered at lakes and streams. The dense forest offered hunting parties scores of deer, elk, beaver, squirrels, and black and grizzly bears, for fur as well as food. Roots for cooking and healing were gathered in the forest as well as the edible inner bark of the hemlock. In the extreme south of the region, they found such starch-rich nuts and vegetables as acorns and camas, a type of wild hyacinth with edible bulbs. For sweeter, tastier food, people could harvest a wide variety of berries: huckleberries, cranberries, strawberries, and other more local varieties such as salmonberry and salalberries.

Scarfaced Charley, a Modoc man from California, shows off his tribal headdress in 1873.

THE PEOPLE

Traditional anthropological and archaeological estimates show that Native Americans came to America over the Bering Land Bridge—now the Bering Straits—between 20,000 and 10,000 years ago. According to the "Land Bridge" theory, they came in search of better land for hunting and gradually worked their way down the west coast. New scholarship on Native Americans places the people of the Pacific Coast and Alaska here much earlier.

Anthropologists estimate that by the end of the eighteenth century, the approximately 176,000 square miles that make up the Pacific Coast from Alaska down to California supported a Native American population of about 150,000 people.

While each tribe had its own dialect and customs, they did trade goods and shared a common sign language. By the age of six, children learned four languages plus sign language. The tribes of the Pacific Coast included the Haida, Kwakiutl, Nootka, and Bella Coola of British Columbia; the coastal Salish of Washington; and the Yurok, Hupa, and Modoc of Oregon and California. The Tlingit and Tsimshian lived along the Alaskan coast.

All these cultures were shaped by the seacoast along which they lived. On the whole, their lifestyles were very similar. For one thing, it was far easier to depend on the abundant sea for food than to try hunting in dense forest, so villages all down the coast were built in sheltered coves, wherever canoes could be safely beached. The tools of every tribe included a wide variety of fish spears, hooks, and harpoons.

SOCIETY

For all the tribes, religion and culture were inextricably linked. Native Americans believed in The Great Mystery, that everything had spirit. God was not a separate entity looking down on them from above. The spirits lived in everything from one's hair to the trees, earth, and mountains. In the coastal tribes of the Pacific Northwest, religious rituals often centered around the spirits of the sea.

Because the sea was so full of food for the taking, including such fish as salmon, which could be smoked and stored without danger of spoilage, the village larders were usually full by the end of summer, leaving the tribes with a good deal of winter leisure time. When people don't have to worry about their survival, they have the leisure time to develop an elaborate cultural life. The Native Americans of the Pacific Coast were no exception.

Native Americans lived in a highly organized society, in which every person had a specific role, yet theirs was a communal lifestyle. Each member of the tribe played a part in contributing to the society, whether as hunter or healer. Children were the responsibility of all members of the tribe. They learned through "discipline games," which taught them language, the proper behavior, and their path in life.

Though each tribe had its leaders and respected members such as the master canoe-builder or

The Pacific Northwest
tribes often caught
salmon in traps, or
weirs. Here a man of the
Ksan tribe in British
Columbia spears the fish
with a gaff.

Priests and healers, the
shamans of the Pacific
Northwest combined
herbal medication with
impressive rituals. A
Tlingit healer exorcises
the evil forces troubling
the patient.

9

Once the salmon were caught, they were smoked or baked and eaten on the spot or stored for later use by drying.

maker of whale-killing harpoons, Native Americans did not know nobility and commoners in the European sense. Most tribes were matrilineal, tracing their heritage through the women of the tribe. They traced their lineage through extended families called clans. In some tribes, careful records were kept to avoid marrying close kin. For example, the Tsimshian of British Columbia, divided the people into four specific matrilineal clans: Wolf, Eagle, Blackfish, and Raven. No one could marry someone from within his or her own clan, which kept the people from worrying about wedding close kin. Strict marriage rules also allowed for social and political ties with those outside their immediate families. Under the Tsimshian system, young boys were raised by their mother's brothers, while girls stayed at home till they were old enough to be married.

RELIGION

Religion for most Native Americans was something to be felt and celebrated on the private, not the public level. Native Americans understood "The Great Mystery." Questions about the existence of God were not asked. You were simply put on Earth to follow a life path, your Earth Walk. This was The Great Mystery.

Storytelling was a tradition common to all Native Americans. The stories were more than entertainment. Storytellers shortened many a damp, dark winter's night by retelling tribal myths, legends, and folktales. They told stories of the creation and of the animals in nature. As with *Aesop's Fables* and other folk tales, the stories often taught the values of the culture. Through storytelling, knowledge was passed from one generation to the next.

The children played "discipline games," in which they learned language and the social mores and morals of their people. Depending on their family, they might learn the healing arts of herbs, or how to tend the fires.

Native Americans have their own stories of creation, of the spirits of the Earth, plants, and sea. Each tribe has its own traditions, yet all share some sense of The Great Mystery. All aspects of the physical world were simply manifestations of different spirits.

Living as they did amid the worlds of dense forest, mountain terrain, and restless sea, the Pacific Coast tribes told stories of the spirits they knew—of birds, volcanoes, ocean, and trees. Some spirits were benevolent to people, or at least indifferent. Others, like the dreadful Cannibal Spirit feared by the Kwakiutl, or the bird-spirit known as Crooked Beak of Heaven, with its love of human flesh, were definitely hostile. These could only be kept at bay through rituals performed by the Shamans' Society.

The shaman—healer, priest, and magician in one—was one of the most important people in any Pacific Coast tribe. He or she interceded with the spirit world, and protected the village from angry spirits or the malice of a witch, a man or woman who, it was believed, secretly practiced sorcery to harm or kill an enemy. Shamans also healed the sick through long, intricate rituals of dance, chanting, and sleight of hand. Both men and women could become shamans, though in such southern tribes as the Yurok, they were almost always female. While there were financial and social rewards to being a shaman, the path to becoming one was difficult. A would-be healer would fast alone for days at a time, praying for aid and dancing ritual dances until, if he or she was fortunate, a spirit helper would appear to set the exhausted fledgling shaman on the proper path.

Throughout their lives, Native Americans practiced rituals, from birth and death to a hunter's secret, individual rites and those associated with the taking of animal life. The first salmon catch of the year, for instance, was greeted as an honored guest so that its spirits would feel kindly towards the tribe and send more salmon its way. Similar rituals were held for the first herring and, of course, the whale. A woman sang her thanks and praise for the charity of the spirits when she stripped cedar bark from a tree. Though the details varied from tribe to tribe, most also held special thanksgiving dances, praising the spirits and asking them to smile upon the people.

The different stages of one's life were ritualized, too. At birth, the newborn and its parents were secluded for a period so that the necessary rituals to protect the baby could be performed. Though not all tribes practiced true coming-of-age rituals, some ceremonies marked the transition from puberty to adulthood. A boy might begin a rigorous routine of ritual bathing and fasting, and set out in search of a guardian spirit. A girl might pass through a period of seclusion, eat only certain foods, even avoid touching her own body during the time of her first menstruation. After a private purification ritual, she would be ready to reenter the world as a woman.

For most tribes, death was viewed as a transformation of a person's spirit. The spirit of the dead person simply was ready to move onto another path. No two tribes felt the same way about the spirit world of the afterlife. The Tlingit tribes saw it as a pleasant place, but difficult for a human spirit to reach. Others thought that when a person died, his spirit stayed near the living to hurry the deceased out of the house by a specially prepared hole in the wall so that a dangerous spirit wouldn't find its way in. Funerary rites varied: Some tribes suspended their dead from trees, others cremated them. A leader's death, of course, demanded special rituals, ending in the spectacular potlatch honoring his memory.

No matter how varied their individual tribal beliefs might be, one spirit was common to all Pacific Coast people: Raven, shape-shifting and unpredictable, neither good nor evil, the force who sets things moving and keeps them stirred up. Some myths say that it was Raven himself who created humanity, others add that it was he who gave those poor, shivering humans fire. All the stories insist that without Raven, life might be a good deal more orderly—but it would also be much less interesting.

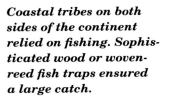

Coastal tribes on both sides of the continent relied on fishing. Sophisticated wood or woven-reed fish traps ensured a large catch.

When more salmon were caught than could be eaten immediately, they were dried on open racks.

Unlike their northern neighbors, the California coastal tribes built their houses of bark and reeds. This model in Point Reyes is part of a reconstructed Miwok village built as an example of living history by local Native Americans.

California coastal tribes also built wooden tepees such as these in Mariposa, California.

THE VILLAGE

A typical Pacific coastal village consisted of up to thirty or more rectangular houses set out in one or two rows in a sheltered cove, just far enough back from the sea's edge to avoid flooding. Rarely more than one story tall, they were built of skillfully cut wooden planks and tied together with stout cords. Their front doors and steeply peaked roofs faced the sea. Most had at least twenty feet of private space surrounding them, with enough room for canoes to be drawn up, covered with matting to keep the sun from splitting the wood.

The floors were usually made of packed earth—though someone of high status might have a more expensive floor of planking. A raised platform for sleeping or sitting, padded with woven cedar bark mats or furs, and sometimes with wooden back-rests, ran the length of the outer walls. The space under the platform served as storage space. Inner walls helped keep out drafts, and probably allowed a little privacy. Central fires, one for each group within the family, were used for cooking and warmth. People named their homes, often giving them grandiose names, such as the Haida house called "Clouds-Sound-Against-It-As-They-Pass-Over."

Each house was home to a single family—including uncles, aunts, cousins, and other kinfolk. A particularly large family might consist of up to 100 people, all of whom had to live in one house. If the family was wealthy enough, they might be able to afford a house up to 600 feet long and 60 feet wide.

A community leader's home, of course, was more elaborate than anyone else's. It included a private apartment, which no one entered without permission and which was screened from the rest of the house by boards painted with his personal crest and protective symbols. Sometimes a stage was built in front of this screen, extending out into the rest of the house, to be used for announcements or proclamations. The closest kin of the leader would also have their private living quarters, screened off by wooden walls.

A NOOTKA WHALE HUNT

The Nootka peoples of Vancouver Island were perhaps the best and most daring hunters on the open sea. In late spring, a whaling expedition would be organized. Crews of eight men in each canoe boldly set out to sea, their faces painted black to show their hunting rage. The streamlined boats cut silently through the waves as they approached their chosen whale. When the steersman gave the signal, the leader of the party would cast a harpoon, tethered to the boat with cedar bark line, with all his strength. The oarsmen would turn the canoe sharply away from the thrashing whale's powerful tail and let the long line attached to the harpoon play out smoothly as the whale dove for safety. When the whale surfaced, the other canoes would close in, chasing it, herding it. More harpoons would be thrown, till at last the whale died and could be towed back towards shore and the waiting village.

Even as they were killing their prey, the men never neglected the proper ritual, thanking the "noble whale" for letting them take it. As they coaxed it towards shore, the men promised the whale great honors. After all, the whale, as with the sea, the land, and all other living beings, had its own spirit. Without properly thanking them, the men might anger the spirits. In the village, the chief's wife kept to her bed until the hunt was over, magically willing docility into the whale. On shore, she first greeted the beached whale, welcoming it to the village with fresh water and sacred eagle down.

Once the whale was properly thanked and the ritual fulfilled, the whale could be butchered. The first and best cuts went to the village leaders. Next, the craftsmen such as the harpoon maker, without whom there could have been no hunt, received their share. After that, everyone received their share of the whale meat. And at last, nothing but bones and tail would remain of the whale.

THE POTLATCH CEREMONY

Perhaps the most famous—if misunderstood—ceremony of the Pacific Coast tribes was the potlatch. At the ritual, the host gained new status or confirmed his power by giving away signs of his wealth. Yet each tribe saw the ceremony in a different way. In all cases, the ceremony celebrated not just one person, but the entire clan. It could take years to properly prepare for a potlatch, which might involve hundreds of guests and last over a week. The suitable gift for every guest, highest to lowest, had to be carefully decided upon. And of course the proper ceremonial songs and dances had

Typically constructed of cedar planks, Pacific Northwest homes of the Nootka tribe housed one or more related families. Totem poles represented each family. Overhead racks held dried fish while shelves for sleeping and storage were built on either side of the house.

While many of the Native American tribes who ground grain used individual metates, or grinding stones, some made use of convenient rocks that served as communal grinding stones. Over time, these rocks would become worn away in spots, as has this example from Tulare, California.

The Pacific Northwest tribes, including the Tsimshian of Alaska, were master woodworkers. This cradle was carved from red cedar with loving care.

to be rehearsed. Meanwhile, the host of the potlatch had to undergo spiritual preparation for a full year, ritually bathing every day before dawn, eating sparingly and, in the final days before the ceremony, practicing total celibacy.

To the Tlingit, a potlatch ceremony might help release a dead chief's spirit from his "Earth Walk" to his next path. The Tsimshian, too, included a potlatch ceremony in their mourning rituals, but for them, it was a chance for the new chief to gather the power due him. The Nootka and Kwakiutl used the potlatch to honor the young man who would someday become chief.

The potlatch itself was a spectacular affair, from the arrival of the guests in a flotilla of canoes to the feasting. Various songs and dances told of clan myths and family sagas, honoring the living and remembering the dead. At last the time came for the distribution of the gifts, each one described lovingly and at length. When this final ceremony was finally over, the host could claim his true high status, granted to him when his guests accepted the gifts.

TOOLS AND BUILDING MATERIALS

A local craftsman carried a sophisticated variety of tools: adzes, hammers, drills, and knives, among other gear, with edges and blades of tough shell, stone, or the regional form of jadeite, and points of horn or bone. River and ocean fishermen used a wide assortment of spears and hooks. These ranged from an ingenious harpoon for whale hunting that was made of bone or horn barbs bound to a wooden shaft and glued into place by a coating of pitch, to deceptively simple fishhooks carved or molded from spruce roots. Shellfish such as clams were gathered at the shoreline with a sharpened stick to dig and pry them out of the sand. To catch salmon more effectively, fishermen would build weirs, or open-work fences, across streams and rivers to divert the fish into traps. Some of these weirs could support catwalks for the hunters, an impressive feat of engineering, particularly when such a weir has been built across a wide, rushing river.

Until recently, it was believed that the people of the Pacific Coast did not use iron tools until the Europeans arrived in the late eighteenth century. Recent finds, however, indicate that Native Americans may have smelted iron long before the Europeans arrived.

Since the tribes lived in the middle of such a densely forested environment, they used wood for just about everything that needed to be built. This included almost all the tools used in the home, from cradles, storage boxes, and chests to bowls and spoons. Even the simplest of these everyday objects shows a love and reverence for wood in every smooth, sophisticated line and bit of intricate carving. Red cedar in the north and the redwood in the south were the woods of choice, because they are the easiest to work, but woodcarvers also worked with other native trees, such as the yellow cedar and the alder. The only woods rarely used by any but the most determined craftsmen were the tougher woods such as fir and hemlock, which are difficult to cut.

A functional Tlingit knife is also a beautiful object in itself. While the steel blade is European, the hilt, with its wood and shell-inlay pommel, reflects Tlingit craftsmanship.

15

A Salish Sho-Ban woman of the Pacific Northwest whirls in a dance that shows off her colorful fringed costume.

CLOTHING AND ORNAMENTS

A wide variety of wood fibers provided Pacific Coast people with clothing. Spruce roots, tough but flexible, were softened by washing and split into strips. The shredded inner bark of red or yellow cedar, sun-dried cattail stalks, and wild cherry bark also were used. Out of these fibers, a weaver could create a variety of water-resistant garments on her half-loom. Shredded cedar bark could be used for women's skirts, complete with a belt around the waist. Red cedar bark made water-repellant rain ponchos or cloaks for men and women, which were frequently edged with fur to prevent chafing. Shredded yellow cedar was woven into robes so soft they needed no lining, and tightly woven, waterproof rain hats. These hats came in many designs, some peaked, some round, and often included designs to indicate the wearer's status. The creative weaver might dye her fibers or add decorations of ornamental grasses and ferns. For trimming and softness, she might also include duck down or prized mountain-goat wool, difficult to obtain for many of the coastal tribes.

Some of the most elegant clothing was crafted from mountain-goat wool. The women of the Chilkat tribe, a division of the Tlingit peoples, weaved goat wool into colorful, intricately patterned fringed robes and shawls (commonly misnamed "blankets"). The weavers followed designs that had been painted onto pattern boards. They wove their fabric in panels, which were then sewn together to create the finished robes. Similar Chilkat robes are still woven in this fashion today.

Some tribes also wore fur cloaks of bear or sea otter skins. Others, such as the coastal Salish, used a very unusual form of wool: They kept a special breed of small, woolly dog specifically for shearing. In the colder regions, such as the Alaskan coastline of the Tlingit tribes, winter garb included long-sleeved deerskin dresses for the women and deerskin trousers for the men.

Because footgear tended to rot quickly on the perpetually damp ground, almost everyone went barefoot during most of the year.

Both men and women of the tribes wore jewelry, and the elegance of their ornaments reflected their status. Necklaces, earrings, headbands, and nose rings of local shells, sometimes with bear claws or bits of fish bone added for contrast, were popular items.

Traders from southern California brought glistening abalone shell pendants, which were more

The Chilkat of the Pacific Northwest wove beautiful robes and blankets from rare mountain-goat wool. Other tribes, who looked on the blankets as status symbols, traded valuable shells and other goods for them. Chilkat robes are still being woven today, though no·longer only by that one tribe. This modern example is by Anna Brown, a Tlingit woman.

brightly colored than the northern shells, to the northern tribes. Some tribes also used copper ornaments, though these, like most native metals, were rare. Nowadays, Native American artists no longer limit their pieces to local materials, and are free to work traditional Northwestern patterns in such nontraditional mediums as gold and silver.

Skin decoration also was popular. In the north, men and women often had their entire bodies covered with intricate tattoos. Tattooing was less popular in the south, though women sometimes had chin tattoos, which were signs of beauty. On holidays, some people enjoyed wearing face and body paint, following the traditional clan designs.

Some Pacific Coast peoples, such as some of the Kwakiutl tribes, flattened or otherwise distorted the shape of the skull. By padding and binding an infant's head, they could reshape the soft bones into what was considered a more elegant line. Though it looks strange to our eyes, it caused no damage to the child's intelligence.

Other creations of the Pacific Coast peoples, considered art today, served a practical purpose. The baskets, trays, and matting woven by all the tribes are beautiful tributes to the craft. Depending on their use—for lightweight storage or heavy

Master weavers, the women of the Pacific Northwest tribes created everything from baskets and mats to rain hats and waterproof clothing from strips of cedar bark. This weaver from the Salish tribe weaves an elegant blanket from mountain goat wool or from the furry dog at her side.

This dramatic Pacific Northwest Early Man statue is from the Provincial Museum in Victoria, British Columbia.

household use—baskets could be made of spruce roots, cedar bark, or grasses. Weavers added dyed grasses or the shiny black stems of ferns into the weave to make even more attractive patterns. Baskets meant for heavy use were so skillfully and tightly woven that they were waterproof, and could even be used as containers for boiling liquids.

Mats were usually woven of red cedar bark, worked in a checkerboard pattern, sometimes with a few dyed strips of red or black added for decoration, and were used indoors and out, as bedding or tablecloths, coverings for beached canoes, and shrouds for the dead.

Ceremonial masks play important roles in Pacific Northwest dance rituals. These masks displayed in the Provincial Museum in Victoria, British Columbia, represent various mythological figures.

A wooden totem symbolizes the Bear Clan of the Tlingit people in Sitka, Alaska. The other major Tlingit family groups included the Eagle, Wolf, and Raven Clans.

specialists in their craft, true artists. Raised by a variation of the post-and-tackle system, the heavy poles stayed in place, without additional support, for about fifty years. Some poles have remained standing for as long as 200 years.

The designs showing ancestral and protective spirits appear on smaller objects as well. Boxes, chests, helmets, and even household items such as spoons repeated the patterns on the totem pole.

BUILDING A CANOE

The sea-going canoe was of vital importance to coastal dwelling Pacific Coast peoples. Thirty or more feet in length, the wooden canoes held eight or more crewmen. Without such a canoe, there could be no deep-sea hunting. The man who could build this large, graceful craft was an honored specialist in each tribe.

The carver usually chose a red cedar tree and cut it down with stone-bladed adzes. With the trunk on the ground, the canoe-builder would begin work by roughing out the shape of the canoe from the tree and removing excess wood to make the trunk light enough for a team of men to drag it to the village. There the craftsman would labor over it alone. Using an adze, he carved out the hull of the canoe. Pouring boiling water in the hull helped soften and shape the wood. Once the basic shape of the canoe was finished, the builder would then carefully add a separate prow and stern to give it added stability on the open ocean.

When the craft had been completed to his satisfaction, the canoe-builder would sand it with scouring rushes and polish it with the rough skin of a dogfish so that it would glide smoothly through the waves. Then he would carve paddles to propel it. Finally, the canoe-builder would decorate the canoe with painting or carving. The canoe could now be launched.

This colorful Tlingit totem pole, carved from painted red cedar, stands in Sitka, Alaska.

THE TOTEM POLE

The totem pole represents the most familiar wooden Pacific Coast object to almost everyone. Though all of them were memorials of a sort, there were several different kinds of pole. Used by the Alaskan and British Columbian tribes, when placed before cemeteries, they honored the dead. When set up in front of a village, they celebrated the village's history and protective spirits. When placed in front of a house, the pole reminded everyone of the owner's ancestry. Those who carved the poles were

BUSINESS MATTERS

Trading among the Pacific Coast tribes centered primarily in the region of the lower Columbia River, conveniently located midway between the northern tribes of British Columbia and Washington, and the southern peoples of Oregon and California. The Chinook tribes lived in this area, and set up a thriving marketplace of furs, slaves, salmon, and shells, which were used for decoration as well as currency. Traders used a common dialect known as "Chinook jargon."

Foremost among businessmen were the Yurok of California. They devised a precise system of grading and valuation for the dentalium shells that were the prime currency of the region. Some of the Yurok men actually had tattooed measurements on their arms for checking the length of dentalium strings. The Yurok had a sophisticated and highly detailed legal code in which each and every possession and right had a specific value. They also had a high percentage of legal disputes.

Not all disputes among the tribes ended peacefully. Raids for goods were an accepted, if unpleasant, fact of life that rarely led to outright war. A feud between two clans, or two tribes, triggered perhaps by a murder, could be bloody indeed. Stone clubs and knives were every bit as deadly as iron or steel, and the warriors fabricated some ingenious armor. Tying a cuirass of wooden rods around the torso protected a man's body, while a wooden helmet complete with a visor, which looked something like the helmets worn by Roman gladiators, protected his head.

Some feuds continued off and on for many years, lasting well into the nineteenth century. Others were settled by peacemaking ceremonies in which the two sides, weary of fighting, would ritually act out combat before a tribal council, then mutually agree to lay down their arms.

SOUTHERN CALIFORNIA: VARIATIONS ON A CULTURAL THEME

Like the more northern tribes of the Pacific Coast, those who lived in southern California depended on the sea for their livelihood. Unlike their northern neighbors, they hunted shellfish and shallow-swimming fish rather than taking to the open ocean. They also had access to acorns which, roasted and ground into flour, provided a valuable source of starch. Like the northern tribes, the peoples of the south were expert weavers and basket makers, and their culture revolved around a form of the potlatch ceremony.

The California tribes differed from their northern

Bight National Historic Park preserves the totems of the Pacific Northwest tribes in Ketchikan, Alaska.

A turn-of-the-century Haida village in the Pacific Northwest illustrates the "front yard" of each family home. Here, where a totem pole marked the family's history and social status, families safely beached their canoes.

neighbors because of their environment. They weren't surrounded by dense forest and carved no totem poles. Their small, relatively simple canoes were crafted from balsawood or reeds. In the milder southern California climate, tribes such as the Yumas and the Mohaves lived in shelters made of brush and woven reeds. These could be easily abandoned whenever a tribe needed to move on. Their next settling place would have abundant supplies for new homes.

Men wore simple breechcloths while women wore skirts or aprons woven from bark or local reeds. They also adorned themselves with tattoos, and boasted elaborate ritual costumes adorned with abalone shell and feathers from the sacred eagle and other birds. The chief of each tribe guarded his people's sacred costumes, and their theft was considered the most terrible of crimes.

Like their northern cousins, the peoples of the south didn't always live in peace with their neighbors. Occasionally two tribes would go to war, usually to avenge a family's honor, fighting with bows and spears and sometimes taking enemy women or children as slaves.

THE OUTSIDE WORLD

Contact with whites, beginning during the eighteenth century, spelled the beginning of the end of an era in Native American history. Trade with whites brought disease and eventually the erosion of tribal culture as whites sought to "civi-

lize" a culture that was thousands of years old.

The Tlingit first traded with the Russians during the eighteenth century. The initial contact was relatively friendly, and the Russians established a permanent trading post in Sitka, Alaska. By the mid-nineteenth century, however, relations with the Russians often deteriorated into bloodshed. Native Americans also now traded fur for iron with British and American ships, and the people, as well as their livelihood—the sea otter—suffered from exploitation.

The ever-increasing trading contacts introduced devastating European diseases such as smallpox, to which the native population had no resistance. The arrival of white settlers, administrators, and missionaries in Washington and Oregon during the mid-nineteenth century resulted in the forced removal of some tribes from their ancestral grounds to reservations far from the coast. The government banned such ago-old customs as the potlatch.

Further south, the Spanish invaded California during the eighteenth century, bringing missionaries with them that abruptly altered the tribal way of life. The new rulers forced Native Americans into the roles of docile servants, outlawing their tribal practices and forcing Christianity on them. A visiting European artist of the time wondered why these people never laughed.

When a new wave of settlers and gold seekers swept over nineteenth-century California, those Native Americans who survived brutality and outright massacre were forced onto barren reservations. A way of life—and very nearly a people—ended with the arrival of white towns and cities.

However, many of the tribes managed to maintain their customs in secret. They could sidestep the potlatch ban, for example, by simply calling the ceremony a "party." The ban imposed by the United States and Canadian governments was not lifted until the 1950s.

Still, the issue of lost Native American lands and broken treaties remains. It wasn't until the mid-twentieth century that some of the Pacific Coast tribes were able to fight for their land in court. In 1961, after negotiations lasting several years, a settlement of over $29 million was granted to the California tribes for outstanding land claims. In 1971, a joint action by Alaskan Native Americans resulted in one of the largest settlements ever: The plaintiffs were awarded forty million acres and nearly $1 billion in compensation for their outstanding land claims.

A cedar Tlingit totem pole in Haines, Alaska, provides a visual record of the various clans of a family's history.

Wearing European clothing, Tsacotna and Natsanitna, two Tlingit girls of the Pacific Northwest, pose rather nervously near Cooper's Point, Alaska, in 1903.

THE GREAT

PLAINS

THE LAND

The vast territory stretching south from Alberta, Canada, into Texas and west from the middle of the Dakotas, Oklahoma, Nebraska, and Kansas to the foothills of the Rockies offered millions of acres of billowing grass to its native inhabitants. The Great Plains, stretching as far as the eye could see, shaped a different Native American culture than that found on the Pacific Coast.

Before white settlers arrived to divide the land into farms and pasture for cattle, most of the land was covered with boundless prairie grasses. In stark contrast, the desolate Black Hills of South Dakota and the butte country of the Dakota Badlands interrupted the Plains. Yet the Missouri and Platte Rivers cut across the Plains, offering a year-

The site of a Sun Dance in Rocky Boy, Montana, is silhouetted against the sunset. Outlawed for a time by the United States government, the ancient ritual of the Sun Dance can now be performed without legal restraint, as it was before the invasion of whites.

round supply of water. Cottonwood and willow trees thrived along the riverbanks, which were home to ducks, geese, and other waterfowl. Forests rich with elm and oak provided food and shelter for a wide variety of animals, including rabbit, deer, antelope, and bear.

The people who lived on the Great Plains most valued the waving sea of grass for its bountiful game. Here was the perfect environment for one of the most famous North American mammals: the American bison, commonly misnamed the "buffalo."

THE PEOPLE

The tribes of the Great Plains have entered American popular culture (in often wildly inaccurate and offensive form) as the "Indians," the stereotypical horsemen of book and screen. In the real world, a variety of tribes lived on the immense sweep of the Plains. Iowa, Omaha, and Wichita are named for Native American tribes, and most would recognize the names Blackfeet, Crow, and Pawnee.

Sitting Bull, the Hunkpapa Sioux chief who defeated General Custer, proudly displays his chief's headdress in 1885. In 1890, police killed Sitting Bull while he was in custody at Standing Rock Reservation in South Dakota.

Other tribes, such as the Mandan and Prairie, are less well known. The name of some tribes, commonly known as the Sioux and Cheyenne, are misnomers attributed to the tribes by French explorers. These tribes were actually the Dakotas, the Native American word for "place of the people of peace."

They followed the buffalo as the great herds grazed on the prairie grass. The buffalo was the source of life for the Native American tribes.

The peoples of the Great Plains all spoke different languages—though they could communicate through a common sign language—and followed different customs, but they have enough characteristics in common to be classed as Plains Indians. Most, like the Crow and Pawnee, were nomadic hunters who followed the buffalo and lived in easily transported tents called tepees. Other Plains tribes such as the Mandan depended on agriculture and trade with other peoples for their livelihood, and lived in settled villages of bark or earthen houses.

Native Americans would say that they inhabited the Great Plains of North America for as long as the land has been there. Archaeological evidence suggests that people may have lived in this part of the country for many thousands of years. More conservative estimates, based on the excavation of "sun wheels"—circular sites cut into the permafrost and marked with stone cairns that may have marked the summer solstice and the changing of the seasons—in the northern reaches of the Plains from Wyoming up into Alberta date to as little as 600 years ago.

Some controversy surrounds the life of these early Plains inhabitants. The fossil record shows that the horse roamed the prairies long before Spanish explorers reintroduced horses to the area during the mid-sixteenth century. For some reason, the horse disappeared. Nomadic tribes may have used the horse, but it had been extinct in North America for thousands of years by the time the Spanish arrived.

The Plains Indians travelled on foot, dragging everything they owned by hand on travois, or wheelless sledges. Some tribes pulled their travois with the only domestic animal available to them, the dog.

SOCIETY, RELIGION, AND RITUAL

Religion and society, the organization of the tribe, were inseparable. In their strict social order, ritual was a part of everyday life. Everyone had a specific role in the community, whether as hunter,

healer, or storyteller. From an early age children heard the stories of creation, of the spirits of the Earth and sky, and of the buffalo they hunted. They learned that knowledge required responsibility, and different ceremonies marked different stages of learning.

Women were the keepers of sacred knowledge, of theology, healing, and social skills, while men had the responsibility to maintain the tribe through survival skills such as hunting. According to one creation myth, woman was created first to make right choices in the life path, man was created to be her companion. In this way, women held the primary responsibility for teaching the values of

daily life, which were considered sacred. The first principle: you must assume responsibility for your choices.

While men led the war parties, for example, they could not return to the village without a ceremonial cleansing. Taking a life, whether human or animal, was a serious spiritual matter. Women would bring the peace pipe for the men to smoke so that they could return cleansed.

Even so, a council of older men, looked up to for their wisdom, governed each tribe. A man or woman could rise to join the ranks of the tribal advisors by brave deeds and wise actions. In addition to the advisors, there were the "police" of

The War Captain looks on at the Feast Day Comanche Dance given at the Tessique Pueblo in New Mexico.

A Cheyenne man from Oklahoma shows off his ritual finery at an Intertribal Ceremonial in Gallup, New Mexico.

28

each tribe who kept the peace. These were members of the various men's societies, such as the Kit Fox or Crazy Dogs, which included most of the able-bodied men of any village. Though there was often keen rivalry between the societies, they took turns in their peace-keeping duties, and saw that village life ran smoothly.

The contraries, the devil's advocates, were warriors who had had a special vision of thunder, commanding them to live their lives backwards. If a contrary, called *heyoka* by the Sioux, said "yes," he meant "no." If he meant to walk forward, he would walk facing backwards. Their role was to question, to challenge people to think about what they said or did. However, a contrary still acted as

bravely—and as "normally"—as any other warrior in the heat of battle.

The shaman also played an important role in tribal life. Trained in a variety of specialties—such as herbs, stomach ills, or mending bones—these healing people employed an impressive array of herbal medicines and rituals to heal the sick. They helped guide the young to moral behavior, and through mystic visions saw where game could be found and what actions the tribe should take. A shaman was born with his or her power, though proper training by an adult shaman and, in some tribes, secret rituals as a member of the Medicine Dance Society, to which only shamans could belong, were needed to properly shape that gift.

Day Star, a Blackfeet woman storyteller, performs for her audience at a Kiowa Pow Wow, or tribal gathering, in Nebraska.

29

In this Mandan hunting ritual, Buffalo Dancers honor and summon the sacred animals.

Working from photographs by James Mooney, Irvin Wright drew an Arapaho Ghost Dance— a ritual to rid the land of white invaders— about 1900.

The Sun Dance, a ritual of manhood, seen here as performed by young Sioux warriors in 1874, was practiced in various forms by many of the Plains tribes. In some versions, a young man danced himself into exhaustion, while others required that the man tear himself free from a rawhide thong run through a slit in his flesh, which was tied to a central pole while he danced.

Colorfully suited Coman- che dancers perform at a tribal gathering at the San Ildefonso Pueblo in New Mexico.

The most common ritual for reaching these powers is known to us as the Vision Quest, in which one found an isolated spot and fasted, praying until a spirit-helper would appear in a vision to show him or her power-objects for the medicine bag. The spirit helper would also provide the proper sacred songs and taboos to guide and help the person through life.

One way in which a man could salute the supernatural powers was by smoking what we know as a peace pipe with his friends or guests. So serious was this ritual that in some of the tribes no one dared enter or leave a tepee till the smoke was completed. The ritual was begun by the man hosting the smoke, ceremonially pointing the pipe stem to the sky, the ground, and the four directions, saying as he did, "Spirit Above, smoke. Earth, smoke. Four cardinal points, smoke." Then he would pray for spiritual help for those within the tepee, smoke the pipe, then pass it around, from right to left, with the sun. The pipe would continue to be passed from hand to hand in silence until all had smoked, or the pipe had burned out. The contents of the pipe varied; the southern tribes used a mixture of sumac and tobacco, while the northern tribes preferred red willow bark and tobacco.

A Hunkpapa Sioux dancer displays his colorful costume.

Wearing a traditional eagle bustle, a Northern Cheyenne prepares to dance at a Cheyenne Pow Wow held in Lame Deer, Montana.

The most important religious ritual for many of the Plains peoples was the Sun Dance, which honored both the sun and the creative force it represented, and celebrated the courage of the warriors dancing it as well. Most of the Plains tribes performed the Sun Dance in a lodge specially built for the ritual with wood and willow branches, though the Sioux danced outdoors.

The Sun Dancers were always men, usually young, who had vowed to dance for personal bravery or for the well-being of their families. Painted in sacred colors of blue, yellow, and green, wearing green willow branches at head, wrist, and ankle, each dancer was given a whistle made from eagle bone. Sometimes the dance was a test of endurance, during which the Sun Dancers danced for four days without sleep or food. In other tribes, the chests of the dancers would be pierced by wooden skewers attached to the lodge's center pole, and they would dance, blowing on their eagle bone whistles to hide any outcries, till the pierced flesh tore free and released them.

The tribes enjoyed other singing and dancing, too. Their musical instruments included rattles

Near Fort Sill, Oklahoma, the shaman Little Big Mouth sits in front of his tepee with his medicine bag about 1870.

Like the prehistoric people who built Stonehenge in England, a tribal group in Wyoming made their own sacred circle marking the seasons of the year. Known today as the Medicine Wheel, it lies near the Bighorn Mountains.

35

Artist H. C. Yarrow drew these Dakota Sioux hoisting a body onto its burial scaffold in 1880.

Near Fort Laramie, Wyoming, the Oglala Sioux perform a tree burial.

This early photograph shows a Native American burial ground on the Great Plains.

made of gourds filled with pebbles and various types of drums, from the larger wooden ones meant to be hit with drumsticks to the small hand drum. Flutes were also used—primarily for coded musical messages between young lovers.

When a boy was considered old enough—emotionally rather than chronologically—he underwent his first Vision Quest, becoming a man if he succeeded in receiving a helpful vision. A girl came of age with the arrival of menstruation; depending on her family's wealth and love, she might be given a feast in her honor, but she would, at least, take part in the ritual of isolation and purification that marked her becoming a woman.

Although some marriages were arranged, young men and women of the Plains tribes often courted each other, fell in love, and sometimes even eloped. If a marriage failed, divorce was possible, both for husband and wife, by the simple means of throwing out the other person's belongings. If a man was sufficiently wealthy, he might consider taking a second wife; instead of hating the idea, the first wife was often glad to have another woman to help share her work.

When a member of the tribe died, close relatives, particularly the women of the family, gashed their arms and legs in a frenzy of grief, and cut off their hair. After the funeral, the family would give away or burn the deceased's possessions, and for an entire year wore old, ragged clothing and covered their faces with ashes. The dead person's name was never spoken again out of respect, and to allow the deceased to rest quietly.

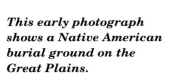

Like most peoples, the Blackfeet of the Great Plains had detailed mourning rituals. Bodies rested on scaffolds, after which the body could be interred in the ground.

Part of Seth East-man's Architect of the Capitol series, Feeding the Dead, *a Plains woman grieves for a loved one, whose body rests on its burial scaffold.*

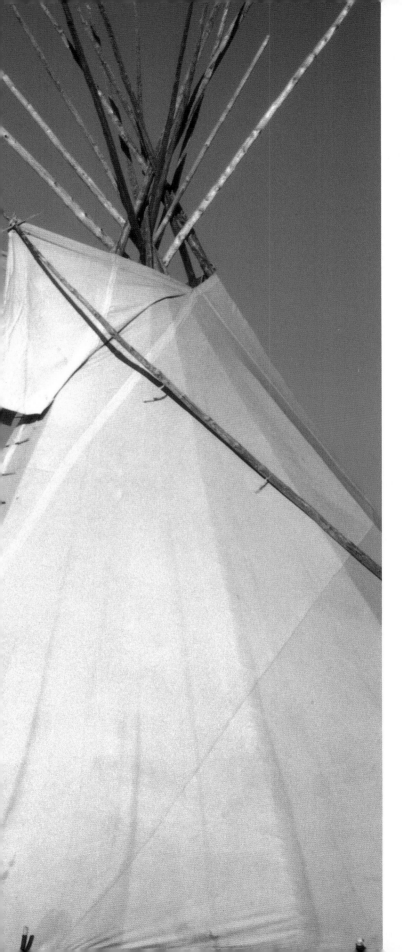

HOME

The tepee was the perfect home for nomads of the Plains. Easy to erect or take down, and easy to transport, the tepee's design was based on those of the tribes of the eastern forests, where it was made of a conical framework of poles covered with birchbark or deer hides. The Plains tepees needed a stronger framework than those of the forests to withstand the strong winds. In the days before the horse, people made do with light fir poles, but with a horse's greater strength, they could use sturdy poles of pine or cedar.

The bark coverings of the east were replaced by the plentiful buffalo hide. Anywhere from six to thirty hides, sewn together carefully with buffalo sinews, made a proper covering. Before a woman could begin work on her tepee, she had to save hides and sinew for as long as two years. When she had the hides, her husband provided fourteen to twenty lodge poles, the number of poles varied from region to region and upon the size of the teepee. Now she could hire the woman in her tribe who specialized in tepee design, paying her and her helpers with a feast and gifts of meat or clothing.

Once the tepee was in place, with the covering pegged down securely and the smoke flaps at the top adjusted to let air in and smoke out, the tepee could be decorated. Porcupine quills and painted murals covered the tepee, and she installed an inner lining to keep in the warmth.

Before the family could move in, the tepee was dedicated with a ritual smoking. The family's belongings—the wife's sewing kit and household tools—were stored in the tepee. The family medicine bag and the hide pouches called *parfleches* that stored the family's clothing hung from the tepee's framework while other items could be stowed

During the early 1830s, the Piegan Plains tribe camp near Fort McKenzie, Montana.

Traditionally painted Blackfeet tepees, erected for a tribal gathering at Browning, Montana, show what teepees in an early twentieth century Blackfeet encampment would have looked like.

The Pawnee, originally inhabitants of what is now Kansas and Nebraska, moved west with the white man. Here, a late nineteenth-century Pawnee family stands by their earth lodge in Loup, Nevada.

Near Fort Dodge, Kansas, in 1870 the Arapaho dry buffalo meat, a vital part of the Plains tribes' diet, on wooden racks.

neatly along the edge of the tepee. The husband's weapons and other war implements were stored in a separate tepee.

The bare ground, partly covered by the family's sleeping furs or, for the Pawnee and Cheyenne with mats woven of rushes, served as the floor. The cooking fire was built in the center of the tepee to warm the entire home and to allow its smoke to rise smoothly through the smoke flaps.

There were variations on the basic theme, of course. The Pawnee preferred lightweight tepees, with a framework of elm or willow saplings for the hot summer days. The Crow used much taller poles than the other tribes, anywhere from twenty-five to forty feet high, so that the crisscrossed ends of the poles towered over the tepee.

The settled agricultural tribes, such as the Mandan, had no use for portable tepees. They preferred permanent wood lodges, low, circular houses covered with earth roofs for insulation.

At twilight, a modern tepee built in the traditional style glows mysteriously from the firelight inside it.

The Minnatarees of the Dakota Territory built earth lodges and wrapped themselves in hide robes to keep warm through the harsh winter.

Members of the Crow tribe built these tepees for a tribal fair, showing how a traditional Crow camp of the past would have looked.

41

The Picture Robe, *by Charles M. Russell, pen and ink and graphite on paper, 1899. As his wife looks on, a Plains man paints a robe that will show a scene from tribal history. In this pen and ink with graphite drawing the artist Charles Russell has romanticized the wife's "pin-up" pose, but knew and respected the Plains tribes.*

At the Pine Ridge, South Dakota, reservation in 1890 the people still lived in tepees. In the foreground, a guard watches over a herd of horses.

The Silk Robe, *by Charles M. Russell, oil/canvas, c. 1890. A Blood Indian tribal leader in Canada sits in the entrance of his tepee, enjoying the twilight. His two wives "flesh" a buffalo hide, preparing it for use as clothing or part of a tepee covering. A particularly finely tanned hide was soft enough to be called a "silk robe."*

This modern-day chief of the Sioux tribes poses in the feather headdress, beaded ornaments, and fringed leggings of his ancestors.

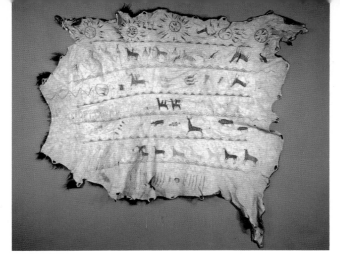

The Sioux painted buffalo robes both for decoration and, in this case, as an easily carried record of the owner's property or family history.

The Native Americans, like most peoples, kept careful track of the seasons. Painted on a buffalo hide by Anko, a Kiowa man, this calendar marks thirteen months between 1889 and 1892.

CLOTHING AND ORNAMENTS

The clothing of all the Plains tribes was made from soft-tanned buffalo or deer skins. Men generally wore a breechcloth, a loose deerskin shirt and snug leggings held up by a belt. Women also wore leggings and long deerskin dresses, often cinched by a belt from which hung such everyday tools as a knife and a sewing kit.

Everybody wore moccasins, simple in the summer, fur-lined in the winter, but the style varied from tribe to tribe. In fact, you could identify a person's tribe from their moccasin design. Women decorated the clothing with leather or hair fringes and lovely needlework of dyed porcupine quills. When contact with white traders made glass beads available, clothing often was adorned with exquisite beadwork. Depending on their husband's wealth and luck in hunting, some women decorated their dresses with elk teeth and trimmed them with fur. People also wore necklaces of bear claws or polished disks of buffalo bone, and earrings of buffalo bone or even shell.

During the late nineteenth century, Great Plains tribes performed the Ghost Dance in a desperate attempt to rid the land of the white invaders. This Pawnee Ghost Dance shirt is made of elaborately fringed buckskin painted with ritualistic symbols.

Whether in necklaces, bola ties, or dance harnesses, modern Blackfeet beadwork is always colorful.

45

This small, lightweight horseman's shield belonged to a Cheyenne warrior. Made of wood and covered with buffalo hide, shields were usually decorated, either by painting alone or, as in this case, by a combination of painted designs and feathers.

The Comanches, like all horse-dependent tribes, designed their baby carriers to protect the baby should it fall from a horse. Heavy padding shielded the baby if the carrier landed on its back, the points over the baby's head stuck into the ground should the carrier fall head-first, and the hood around the baby's face protected it if the carrier fell face down.

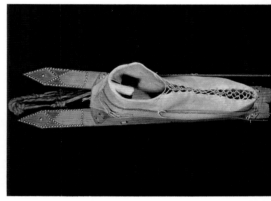

This Cree man, dressed in traditional tribal finery and wearing a contemporary version of a Mandan eagle-feathered headdress, poses before a modern-day tepee set up during a celebration in Elmo, Montana.

47

This painting by George Catlin reflects the Crow tribes' pride in their hair. Both men and women wore it long and flowing.

A little Comanche girl wears her Feast Day finery and face paint for her place in the tribal Comanche Dance at the San Juan Pueblo, New Mexico.

Two Blackfeet warriors show off their finery in this nineteenth-century photograph. Note the beadwork and painted designs for both rider and horse.

The sacred smoking of a ritual pipe is common to many Native American tribes. These Blackfeet pipes are elaborately carved and decorated.

Curley Bear, a Blackfeet chief, was photographed in 1903 wearing these elegant ermine ornaments.

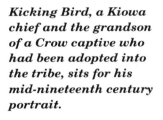

Kicking Bird, a Kiowa chief and the grandson of a Crow captive who had been adopted into the tribe, sits for his mid-nineteenth century portrait.

THE BUFFALO

Literally every aspect of Plains life from birth to death included some use of the vital buffalo. A Plains baby was first swaddled in a blanket made from the skin of a buffalo calf, and grew up in tepees made of buffalo hide. Scraping, soaking, and rubbing with a mixture of buffalo fat and brains by patient, hard working women softened other hides till they could be cut and sewn into all the clothing needed by the family, from leggings, dresses, and shirts to moccasins and gloves. Hides taken in late autumn, covered with thick, warm winter fur, were transformed into winter robes and blankets. A thick piece of hide might become the face of a warrior's shield, while extra pieces of hide could be used as the heads of drums. Rawhide strips cut from buffalo hide served whenever good, sturdy rope was needed, or in the manufacture of saddles and bridles. Tails became fly whisks, and hair stuffed pillows, cradle boards, and balls. Horns were turned into drinking vessels or carved into spoons. The buffalo's bones became knives or useful tools for fleshing yet more buffalo hides, or even dice, and the buffalo's hoofs and scrotum found a new use as rattles for sacred dances.

Buffalo meat, of course, was a mainstay of life, roasted, stewed, or, in the case of certain choice bits such as the liver, eaten raw. To add flavor, sometimes the meat was cooked over a hickory fire. Particularly tough portions could be boiled in a pit lined with a clean skin, and filled with water and hot stones. Whatever meat wasn't eaten immediately could be sun dried as jerky or pounded together with berries and fat to make the high-protein, high-energy, lightweight food known as *pemmican*.

The marrow, sometimes with savory herbs added for flavoring, was often turned into the filling of sausages cased in cleaned sections of buffalo intestine, while the cleaned stomach of the buffalo served as an excellent cooking pot. The dinner within that pot would almost certainly be cooked upon a fire of dried buffalo chips.

When a member of the tribe died, the buffalo provided one final gift: The corpse would be wrapped in a shroud made from buffalo hide.

Plains tribes relied on buffalo for food, clothing, and shelter. In the Architect of the Capitol series, Buffalo Chase, *an 1868 painting by Seth Eastman, a rider chases his prey on horseback.*

51

THE BUFFALO HUNT

Since the buffalo hunt was of such vital importance to the Plains tribes, it's not surprising that it was begun with prayer and ritual and timed carefully to coincide with the annual migration of the herds. Scouts set out first, seeking a herd, judging its size and strength, then bringing the news to the rest of the hunters, who waited downwind so the buffalo wouldn't scent them. No matter how excited those hunters might be, longing to attack the precious herd, they kept themselves under rigid control. The hunters knew only too well that a mistake by one man could mean a poor hunt,

disaster for everyone, and punishment for the hunter who made the mistake.

As they waited, the men stripped themselves and their horses of any extra gear, making themselves as lightweight as possible. When at last the signal for the attack was given, each rider charged forward at top speed, bow or lance ready. The specially trained buffalo horses gave their riders clear targets as they darted in and out among the heavier, dangerous buffalo. A misstep or a fall would mean the death of horse and man under trampling hoofs.

The women followed the hunt with pack horses,

waiting for the signal to approach. They would skin and butcher the slain buffaloes, each woman identifying her husband's prey by the designs painted on his arrows. Among some tribes such as the Cheyenne, men butchered their own kills and brought them back to the village for the women to prepare.

During the butchering, a boy who had made his first kill would be honored. He would be offered the tongue of his buffalo, considered the tastiest part. In turn, the boy would give away the tongue, showing his generosity. He wouldn't taste the meat of his buffalo either, as that would have showed his greed.

The Great Buffalo Hunt, **by William Robinson Leigh, 1947, oil on canvas, photographed by James Milmoe.**
After horses arrived on the Plains with the Spanish in the sixteenth century, the Plains tribes no longer had to depend on the long, laborious tracking of buffalo on foot. Riding in hunting parties on trained buffalo horses, hunters swooped down on their prey, making as many kills as necessary for the needs of the tribe. (This image has been cropped.)

Indian Women Moving, **by Charles M. Russell, oil/ canvas, 1898.**
Plains tribes led a nomadic life, following the buffalo herds. At dawn on moving day, the women took down the tepees and packed their family belongings onto the horse-drawn travois. The camp's dogs circle alertly about the riders in this painting by "cowboy artist" Charles Russell.

On the Trail in Winter, **by Henry Francois Farny, 1894, gouache, photographed by Charles Swain.**
A small Plains tribal party, bundled up against the bitter cold, follows a trail through the snow-covered Rocky Mountains. (This image has been cropped.)

54

THE RETURN OF THE HORSE

Before the Spanish conquistadors led by Francisco Vasquez de Coronado crossed the southern Great Plains in 1541, the nomadic Plains peoples followed the buffalo herds for at least a thousand years. The Spanish reintroduced the horse to the Great Plains, radically changing the Native Americans' way of life.

Recognizing the horse's value for hunting and travelling, the tribes took up the fine art of horse stealing, aided by the fact that some horses had already liberated themselves from their Spanish owners and were running wild on the Plains in ever-increasing numbers. The horses rapidly reproduced, creating the first herds of what were later to be known as mustangs: small, tough, and of seemingly endless endurance. By the late seventeenth century, the Spanish complained that literally thousands of mustangs ran wild—and thousands were being stolen all over the Southwest and the Great Plains. Less than 100 years after Native Americans had seen their first horses, the tribes' slow, pedestrian lifestyle had vanished forever.

THE HORSE IN PEACE AND BUSINESS

Horses were always privately owned among the Plains tribes; there weren't any communal herds. But the animals are expensive to keep properly tended, fed, and watered. A wealthy man by Plains standards might own thirty or more horses. The animals were considered the prime "coin" for trading or wagering. They were often given or lent to the poorer members of the tribe as acts of charity, or offered to someone of equal or superior status in thanks for favors granted or as gifts of honor. They were also an expensive part of the proper bride price for a wife, whose father might insist on a prospective groom offering a high number of horses, indeed, to ensure that only the very best of providers might win his daughter.

It wasn't only the men of the Plains tribes whose lives were made easier by the horse. The women usually owned their own horses, which gave them a certain amount of freedom. Sometimes they would participate in horse races or, like the Comanche or Sioux, ride out to hunt antelope and other game. While women seldom gained any new horses by taking part in raids (unless they were helping their husbands), women in tribes like the Blackfeet eagerly added to their private herds by careful trading.

The horse freed the tribes of the Great Plains to travel great distances with relative ease. When hitched to a travois, or horse-drawn sledge, the horse carried a family's possessions when they moved.

The Sign of Peace, *by Henry Francios Farny, 1908, oil on canvas, photographed by James Milmoe. The feathers in his hair and in his mount's forelock mark the bravery of this proud Plains warrior. With his leather shield slung over his back, he raises his arm in a gesture of peace. Although the artist has painted him with right arm raised, the traditional peace sign was made by raising the left arm, closest to the heart.*

55

The coming of horses caused yet another major change in the economy of the Plains: Their use gave the nomad hunters, with their easy mobility, dominance over the once-superior farming tribes. Those peoples, such as the Mandan who remained farmers, found themselves surrounded by the horsemen, frequently trapped within their village walls. It was an excellent incentive for tribes like the Cheyenne to abandon their farms, seize themselves some horses, and convert to a nomadic way of life.

RAIDING AND WARFARE

Horse raiding on other tribes was raised to a fine art among the peoples of the Great Plains. Here was an opportunity to make a poor man wealthy, a wealthy man richer yet, and give a youngster his first initiation into proper warrior behavior. The raid began with a ritual. During the drumming ceremony the night before, the raiders sang of the horses they planned to steal and prepared their

weapons and their war medicine bundles, each of which contained objects sacred and significant to the individual warrior holding it. In the morning, the raiders (usually all male, though sometimes a husband and wife team would work together) would set out for the enemy camp, led by the warrior who had planned the raid, possibly inspired by a dream. The warriors would normally be on foot, so their horses wouldn't give them away by whinnying at a dangerous moment. The actual raid took place at night, and if the raiders were clever and lucky, they would get away with their prizes before an alarm could be sounded.

Outright warfare was just as dangerous as raiding. Whether the tribes dueled over honor or the right to hunt buffalo on certain lands, a battle was much easier to wage from horseback. Warriors fighting on foot had used a large, bulky shield and awkward rawhide armor. A mounted warrior needed only a small shield and bow, and could discard his armor in favor of speed, charging down on a foe to fight him hand to hand.

There was great honor to be gained in combat, from the taking of the enemy's horse and scalp to the most honorable act of all: the counting of coup, the touching of a foe. While coup could be counted against anyone of the enemy tribe, adult or child, or even against enemy property, the highest honor went to the warrior who touched an enemy in the heat of battle, called counting coup. There were rigid rules attached to counting coup. If a warrior wounded his foe from afar before touching him, no coup was awarded. If, however, one of the enemy managed to touch a warrior, that warrior was shamed. A man who had counted coup successfully was expected to recount his feat to a tribal council, who might call in witnesses to support his claim. If everyone agreed he had counted coup, the warrior would be awarded a coup feather from a golden eagle.

Women had their place in warfare, too. The proud wife performed the scalp dance, displaying her husband's war trophies, and boasting his prowess before the camp. It was the mourning of a woman whose husband or son had been slain by the foe that prodded the warriors to take revenge, though sometimes a widow might confront a war leader with a sacred smoking pipe and force him and his warriors to take action for her.

Touring artist Karl Bodmer portrayed these Teton Sioux horsemen showing off their agility during the early 1830s.

The Smoke Signal, *by John Mix Stanley, oil on canvas, 1868, photographed by James Milmoe.*
The tribes of the Great Plains communicated across the vast distances of the region with carefully controlled smoke from signal fires in a form of shorthand.

Although artist Karl Bodmer seats this Blackfeet warrior on an Arabian horse, rather than the wiry range horse of the Plains, this portrait from the 1830s depicts a Plains warrior in full regalia.

The White Cloud, Head Chief of the Iowas, *by George Catlin, c. 1844/1845; National Gallery of Art, Washington; Paul Mellon collection. Renowned nineteenth-century artist George Catlin protrays this important man of the Iowa tribe in all his finery, providing an invaluable record of hair and clothing styles.*

Not all women were content to play a supporting role in warfare. Many of the tribes, including the Sioux, Crow, and Cheyenne, tell of great female warriors who counted coup, received the honorable eagle feathers, and danced and sang with the other warriors. The Cheyenne Buffalo Calf Road Woman rode full-tilt into the heat of battle to rescue her fallen brother. Running Eagle, a Blackfeet woman, was famous as a warrior, war chief, and holy woman.

A warrior would paint himself and his horse for battle. He would paint symbols on his horse that meant "an enemy killed" or "a successful horse raid," decorate the mane and tail with eagle feathers, and tie scalps to the bridle. Some riders became so skilled, they could slide down one side of their galloping horse, hook a leg over the animal's back, and free their hands for their bows while presenting a small target for the enemy.

HUNTING AND FARMING

Although the buffalo was the primary animal in the Plains tribes' diet, other animals such as deer and antelope were hunted as well. Some tribes also ate small game, such as prairie dogs and rabbits, and most included some of the so-called game birds, such as wild turkey and quail in their diets. Salt was the seasoning of choice, scraped up from natural salt beds or condensed from salt springs.

The tribes' menu also included the many summer and autumn fruits available on the Plains, such as wild currants, blackberries, wild cherries, and strawberries. Some of the fruit was eaten fresh, but a good portion was sun dried and stored by the women for the lean winter months. Vegetables such as lamb's quarters—rich in iron and vitamins—and wild potatoes also were gathered by the women. A sweet tooth could be satisfied by honey from hives of wild prairie bees.

The settled tribes, like the Mandan, living in their fortified villages along the Missouri, depended more upon agriculture than the hunt. They traded their deliberately grown surplus of cornmeal and beans for finely dressed hides and buffalo robes from the nomadic tribes. The Mandans were good traders, often stripping their nomadic cousins of more trade goods than the nomads had intended. However, the promise of fresh corncakes and bread to supplement a meat-rich hunter's diet must have sweetened a few tempers.

Big Soldier, or Wahktageli, a Dakota chief, sat for his portrait in 1833. Note the elaborate fringe and ornamented leggings that decorate Big Soldier's costume.

Four Bears, an early eighteenth-century Mandan chief, stands in full warrior regalia. During the mid-1800s smallpox brought by the Europeans decimated the Mandan people.

Part of the Architect of the Capitol series, Dog Dance of the Dakotas, *by Seth Eastman portrays the ritual dance of a Sioux warrior society in 1868. Members of such a society followed a strict code of ethics and honor.*

Pehriska-Rupa, a member of the Hidatsa tribal warrior society known as the Dog Band, displays his ritual costume.

"See-non-ty-a", an Iowa Medicine Man *by George Catlin, c. 1844/1845; National Gallery of Art, Washington; Paul Mellon Collection.*
Dressed in his fine shell jewelry, the wise, aging shaman See-non-ty-a of the Iowa tribes sits proudly for his portrait.

At a Blackfeet Pow Wow, tribal elders proudly display signs of their dual heritages, as United States citizens and as members of their tribe.

The Southern Cheyenne Stump Horn and his family pose in front of their home with a horse-drawn travois in this turn-of-the-century photograph.

Red Cloud, chief of the Oglala Sioux, posing with a European cane in his hands.

THE COMING OF THE WHITE MAN

The first contacts—other than the brief excursions of the Spaniards in the sixteenth century—were relatively peaceful trading and trapping ventures in the early nineteenth century. Unfortunately, the Mandans were soon to suffer from these meetings, which introduced smallpox. Having no resistance to the disease, they were swiftly and tragically decimated. By 1837, only 127 Mandans remained. The nomadic tribes, able to escape regions harboring illness, suffered less from disease than from two other manmade plagues: the slaughter by white hunters of the buffalo for hides or sport, and the hunger of white settlers and cattlemen for new land. Warfare, far more bitter than any honorable horse raid or swift, coup-taking battle, and atrocities performed by white and Native American alike, all too soon became the norm for the Plains tribes. Even with such temporary victories as Little Bighorn, and such desperate rituals as the Ghost Dance, a ceremony aimed at creating a mystic world without white men, the traditional world of the Plains was doomed.

Even after crushing military defeats and the desperate poverty of reservation life, the spirit of the Plains tribes remains alive. Political actions such as the 1971 occupations of Alcatraz Island and the village of Wounded Knee by armed Sioux militants focused America's attention on the plight of the Plains peoples. Court actions such as the successful 1961 lawsuit by the Crow reservation in Montana against the United States government for lands unjustly taken netted the reservation about $9 million. A similar suit in 1964 by the Cheyenne resulted in an award of about $3.9 million. With these continued efforts, the people of the Great Plains are making themselves heard. And the ancient spirit of the tribes lives again as young generations of Native American children discover new pride in their roots.

A famous chief in his own right, Quanah Parker was the son of a Comanche chief and his white wife. Here he poses in front of a tent toward the end of the nineteenth century.

TRIBES OF
THE GREAT BASIN
AND PLATEAU

THE LAND OF THE GREAT BASIN

The Great Basin covers over 200,000 square miles of grim desert scrub land and salt flats in what is now Nevada, Utah, the western edge of Colorado, and the southern portions of Washington and Idaho. For over a million years, this has been a hot, arid land, cut off from eastbound rain clouds by the towering Sierra Nevadas to the west. The very air seems to shimmer from the dry heat.

Despite its name, the Great Basin is actually a series of valleys ridged by ancient, eroding mountains. Millions of years ago, the Basin was a great inland sea filled with the waters of melting glaciers. The desert heat gradually evaporated that sea, leaving behind only a few small pools, streams, and the occasional marsh.

Orian Box, a Southern Ute artist in Ignacio, Colorado, creates colorful designs with symbols of the old and new Native American in his art work.

THE PEOPLE OF THE GREAT BASIN

Such a harsh landscape couldn't support a very large population, or a large concentration of people in one place. Still, a good many widely scattered tribes with similar ways of life and speaking different languages, or at least different dialects, called the Great Basin home. These tribes included southern branches of the Shoshone and Paiute, who were related through their languages, though they couldn't understand each other, the Utes, after whom Utah is named, and the Washos.

The lives of the Great Basin tribes were intimately tied to the turn of the seasons. The scarce rainfall and uncertain surface water made farming impossible, and larger game such as antelope rarely entered the region. The tribes of the Great Basin became master foragers, learning not to depend on any one source of food. Since the expected crop of pinon nuts or usually dependable desert pool might fail them at any time, they took advantage of every possible edible plant and animal. What they ate varied with the season.

During the spring, tribes often camped at the edge of a marsh, where the women would harvest the first young cattails for their edible stalks and tubers. The men lured ducks returning to the north with carefully carved decoys and snared them in nets woven of grass cords. Women gathered duck eggs from nests along the shore, while men set out in reed rafts to harvest those eggs not reachable from dry land.

As the year ripened into summer, the tribe would move down to the sparse desert rivers now full from the melting snow miles away, and swarming with newly hatched fish. As quickly as the men could spear them, the women would gut the fish and hang them on wooden frames to dry.

By full summer, the tribe would move into the hills, away from the intense heat of the Basin floor. Men and women gathered whatever edible plants they could find, from watercress to elderberries and thornbush berries. They also harvested seeds and grain from such plants as rice grass, which the women winnowed in their woven grass baskets and then ground into meal.

Once every decade or so, enough pronghorn antelope might appear in the Basin for a hunt. The tribe's shaman worked out the details. On his instructions, a holding pen would be woven out of wood in what his incantations and common sense told him was the proper place, and the men would drive the antelope towards it, praying that the swift little animals—capable of speeds up to sixty miles an hour—wouldn't escape. If the shaman's magic and the tribe's luck held, the antelope would be trapped in the pen, where the men could kill them with spears and arrows.

As the year turned towards autumn, the small, scrubby pine trees produced an eagerly awaited harvest of pinon nuts. This was one of the few times when the smaller tribal groups gathered together to share the harvest and exchange news and gossip. It was also a time for young men to meet and court young women from outside their immediate group. Men harvested the nuts by shaking down the pine cones with hooked sticks while boys who were light enough climbed the trees and picked the cones. The women and girls gathered and husked them, and stored them in finely woven grass baskets. Sometimes the nuts were roasted and ground, then boiled into a nutritious soup. Once the harvest was completed, the tribes would go their separate ways again, not to meet until the next year's harvest.

With the coming of full autumn, the worst of the heat on the Basin floor lessened enough for the tribes to come down from the hills in search of small game. The jackrabbit was the preferred source of meat, and highly important to the tribes as one of the only sources of fur. The men took no chances with the hunt. Rather than each man trying to kill his own prey, a tribe would set up their cord nets in a vast semicircle, then frighten the rabbits into them. The younger men and boys were agile enough to kill them with clubs and arrows as they ran, while the older men waited by the nets to kill the animals that would get entangled.

But the desert world is fickle. There might not be a large enough rabbit population each year. The tribes pragmatically caught whatever game they could, including kangaroo rats, gophers, ground squirrels, and mice, and whatever birds, such as flickers and robins, they managed to snare. Lizards, too, were eaten, and the occasional swarms of protein-rich locusts, grasshoppers, and ants were seized upon with delight, roasted and ground into flour.

Winter was harsh on the desert, cold and raw, with chill winds sweeping down on the tribes. The gathering of food was nearly done for the year, although men would still hunt the small burrowing animals such as ground squirrels, flooding them out or digging them up from their burrows with sticks.

In 1877 the Nez Perce surrendered to the United States Army. One of their chiefs, Looking Glass, posed in front a tepee.

A modern Shoshone young man and his horse show off the ritual trappings of an honorable Shoshone warrior and his favorite mount.

Two nineteenth-century brush-and-hide lodges sit in the harsh desert landscape of the Great Basin.

HOME, CLOTHING, AND THE TOOLS OF DAILY LIFE

Like all nomads, the people of the Great Basin built for mobility, not permanence. A home in warmer weather might consist of a simple cone made of willow poles and covered with bundles of reeds, comfortable enough when a family was gathered within around a fire, sheltered from the chill of the desert night. When the family moved on, it would leave this temporary, easily replaced shelter behind. Winter homes were basically the same, although the reed bundles were thicker, leaving no gaps save for the opening and the smoke hole in the shelter's roof.

In the height of the summer heat, people wore very little: breechcloths of woven grass for the men and short reed skirts for the women. For cooler weather or the chilly nights, women wove pounded sagebrush and cedar bark into sleeveless shirts and pants for the men and blouses and skirts for the women. Winter clothing included rabbit skin cloaks, painstakingly made from long spirals of fur woven around plant fiber for warmth. About 100 strips made a cloak large enough for a man. Though the tribes usually went barefoot, they did sometimes wear bark or animal skin moccasins if the weather was particularly bitter.

The tribes of the Great Basin excelled in basket making, weaving containers of grass, reeds, and willow bark—often including different fibers in one basket to create a pleasing two- or three-toned design—that were so tightly made that even the finest flour wouldn't sift through. They also weaved cattail and tulle reed mats to make their homes more comfortable. Twine made from the milkweed plant, chokecherry branches, and twigs could be woven into cradles for babies, which were then covered with precious antelope hide.

SOCIETY AND RITUAL

Since Great Basin tribal groups were so small, consisting sometimes of only one family or a few related families, their social structure was less rigid than other Native American tribes. Family ties were kept strong by intermarriages; sometimes a man might wed two sisters, or a brother and sister of one family might marry a sister and brother of another. Women held a cherished place in Great Basin society, both as efficient foragers and weavers and as nurturers of the tribe's young. It was not uncommon for one woman to have two or more husbands.

The Great Basin tribes didn't have a rigid hierarchy of leadership, though the elders would be turned to for advice. A tribe's shaman was a healer, someone who had been granted knowledge by the animal powers through dreams. Anyone who had such power dreams could become a shaman, there were no special rites or privileges involved.

Everything that existed, the Great Basin tribes believed, was intertwined, part of the supernatural force, the *puha*. Whenever they took something from the Earth, whether an animal or a plant, they returned something, even if it was only a pebble. One of the major rituals of the tribes took place when they gathered to harvest pinion nuts, and included prayers and a sacred dance that lasted through the first night of gathering, during which the singers would offer up songs of thanksgiving.

THE GOLD RUSH

The California gold rush spelled the downfall for the tribal way of life. Though the first gold diggers had little impact, they were closely followed by hordes of settlers. The discovery of gold and silver in Nevada brought a new rush into the region, and with it a devastating blow to the fragile Great Basin ecology. White settlers cut down the precious pine trees, and their horses and cattle destroyed the grasses. Diseases such as cholera decimated the tribes, and the survivors found themselves pushed onto reservations after the United States government laid claim to the Great Basin.

Nowadays, some of the descendants of the Great Basin tribes are taking a belated revenge. The Paiutes are developing tourist facilities on their lands to earn money from white sightseers. In 1950, the Utes won a $31 million lawsuit against the United States for the land that was forcibly taken from them but never paid for. They now are in the process of leasing the rights to oil found, ironically, under the reservations onto which they were forced.

A Shoshone-Bannock woman dancer, wearing an elaborately fringed costume, stretches out her arm in a ritual gesture.

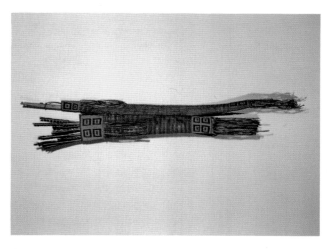

A quiver and bow case from the Bannock tribes of the Plateau region has suffered the ravages of time, but still illustrate the tribe's fine beadwork designs.

Belonging to Chief Joseph of the Nez Perce tribe, this rifle case is finely decorated with beadwork designs and rawhide fringes. Arrow quivers were similarly adorned before the first rifles were brought into the region.

69

THE LAND OF THE PLATEAU

The land lying to the north and northwest of the Great Basin is so different, it could almost be another world. Bordered by the Cascade Range to the west and the Rocky Mountains to the east—which on a modern map includes parts of British Columbia and Alberta, Washington, Oregon, Montana, and Idaho—much of the Plateau lies at a fairly high altitude. Unlike the Great Basin, rain isn't blocked by the mountains to the west. The Plateau region is a land of contrasts, of swift rivers such as the salmon-rich Columbia, rushing westward to the Pacific Northwest, of near-desert plains to the south and subarctic prairie to the north, of soaring mountains and high, fertile valleys lush with vegetation feeding moose, bear, and large herds of deer and elk.

The Plateau fed a wide variety of people as well. Though much of the territory was either too high or too arid to support enough vegetation for a heavy population, an assortment of tribes did migrate from surrounding regions. These people had cultural and linguistic ties to the tribes in the lands all about them, from the Pacific Coast to the Plains, from the subarctic to the Great Basin. This mixture made the Plateau an anthropological melting pot of customs and cultures.

THE PEOPLE OF THE PLATEAU

It has been estimated that the 1,200 mile journey along the Columbia River to the Pacific Ocean a traveller passed over thirty different tribes. The earliest of these diverse peoples apparently arrived in the Plateau region shortly after the last Ice Age (about 10,000 years ago), drawn to the fish-filled Columbia River. The Dalles-Deschutes region, approximately 150 miles inland, still an important salmon fishing area, shows a clear archaeological history dating back to 9,000 B.C. Successive waves of immigrants brought ever new languages and customs to the Plateau area. By about 1,000 B.C., the ancestors of such tribes as the Bannock, Nez Perce, Northern Shoshone, Walla Walla, and Yakima were already settled in the region.

SOCIETY

Since the Plateau was crossed by such broad waterways as the Columbia and Fraser Rivers, it was the center of a thriving trade between the people who lived near the rivers and those of the Pacific Coast. Merchants came from the coast in their large cedar canoes, bringing rich otter pelts

and exotic shells, which they bartered with the Plateau peoples for deerskin and basket making materials. The amount of river traffic was overseen by the Chinook tribes, who occupied the terrain midway between the Pacific Coast and the Plateau. Shrewd traders, they often levied tolls on canoes passing through their territory. Since no two tribes spoke a common language, trading was carried out in the Chinook jargon.

Though more fertile than the Great Basin, the Plateau region couldn't support vast numbers of people living together in any one place. As a result, most of the Plateau tribes, like their neighbors to the south, were made up of small, semi-nomadic bands, sometimes little more than extended families. As with the tribes of the Great Basin, such small groups didn't need a rigid social structure. Each Plateau tribe was led by an elder, or advisor, a wise man chosen for the job because the rest of his people respected him. Some of the larger tribal groups, such as the Nez Perce and the Coeur d'Alene, were more strictly organized, staking out their territory and punishing trespassers on their hunting grounds. Other larger tribes such as the Kootenai needed a council of elders to rule on disputes and wrongdoing within the group. Anyone found guilty of breaking tribal law might be punished by flogging. Most of the other Plateau peoples, though, ignored the concept of private tribal territory, and left the punishment of wrongdoers to the families involved.

HOME

Plateau homes varied from tribe to tribe, and echoed the influence of both the Pacific Coast peoples and those of the Great Plains. Some of the Northern Shoshone, who lived in what is now Idaho, had easy access to forests and built plank houses similar to those of the Pacific Coast tribes. The Northern Shoshone, who lived closer to the Great Plains, preferred the Plains-style tepee instead. Tribes such as the Kootenai, Nez Perce, and other Plateau tribes used the tepee in the summer, but sometimes built more permanent longhouses made of a framework of poles covered with woven mats to live in for the rest of the year. Many of the other tribes had two different types of home as well, digging out earthen lodges with roofs of wood or sod—well-insulated against the cold—for their winter homes, and constructing simple huts of bark, brush, or woven reeds for the summer.

Usually the floors of winter homes or semi-

Leaders of the Plateau tribes show off their finery, which includes elaborate headdresses indicating their rank.

Umapine, a chief of the Cayuse tribe, displays his spectacular feather headdress and elaborately beaded and ornamented clothing in this 1909 photograph.

A man of the Yakima people and a Shoshone-Bannock woman, both from the Northwestern United States, display their tribal costumes at a Fort Hall Pow Wow.

71

A bright-eyed Paiute baby stares in astonishment at the camera from his cradle board.

The Athabascan people live in the northernmost region of the Plateau, within the Yukon Territory and inland Alaska. The Athabascan still trap beaver for their pelts.

permanent houses were lined with mats and strips of bark, though the floors of homes in the higher hills would often be carpeted thickly with boughs of fir or balsam. A layer of matting or animal skins was placed under the family's bedding.

In the smaller tribes, lodges were usually set up wherever the owners wanted them. But in tribes like the Kootenai, where there would be enough people to form a genuine village, the chief would be the one to decide where homes should be placed. His would be in the center of an arc, with the homes of the subchiefs flanking it, the next important families on either side of those, and so on, down to the outer ends of the arc.

The Plateau tribes kept accurate family records. It was a woman's job to keep the history of her own family, which she did with a "time ball," a length of twine knotted to mark important events. A time ball was considered a valuable family artifact, and was often buried with the woman who had kept it.

HOUSEHOLD GOODS AND TOOLS

Just as house styles varied from tribe to tribe, so did the household goods. Many Plateau peoples, influenced by the Pacific Coast tribes, were expert weavers and basket makers, working with shredded barks and grasses to create everything from tightly woven cooking vessels and trays to mats for floors and walls, and snowshoes for the heavy snows of Plateau winters. Other tribes, like the northern Kootenai, made snowshoes but weren't basket makers at all. Instead, they traded clay pots with the Nez Perce and Coeur d'Alene for woven baskets. The Northern Shoshone also occasionally made clay pots, and carved other pots and pipes from steatite.

Instead of worrying about cooking pots, the Flathead and Kootenai used a simple, ingenious method to boil their dinners. A hole was dug and lined with rawhide. They poured water into the hole and dropped hot stones from the fire in to boil the water.

Though some evidence shows that Native Americans did use iron, most Plateau tribes used such easily flaked and sharpened stones as glossy black obsidian or chert, the North American form of flint, for knife blades and arrowheads. They crafted a wide variety of tools from the bones and antlers of deer or buffalo, from awls and needles to picks and hide scrapers. The Flathead and Kootenai tribes were famous as makers of elegant, powerful compound bows, made of thin, supple layers of wood or laminated mountain sheep horn. These bows were so highly rated among the Plateau and Plains tribes that the going price of one was a valuable horse.

CLOTHING

Plateau clothing styles closely resembled that of the Plains Indians. Although some of the Plateau tribes did experiment with robes of woven bark, such as the Pacific Coast peoples wore, the material of choice was usually finely tanned buffalo hide or deerskin, prepared and softened by the women of the tribe. A typical man's costume consisted of a breechcloth and leggings supported by a belt, a long shirt reaching to about the hips, and moccasins. A woman wore knee-length leggings, an ankle-length dress held in by a belt, and moccasins. She might also carry a "handbag" of woven bark or grass. Like the Plains tribes, the Plateau people adorned their outfits with fringes and designs, either painted on or embroidered with dyed porcupine quills.

Unlike the Plains tribes, both men and women of the Plateau tribes wore woven caps pointed like fezzes, often decorated with feathers. In the winter, they wore warmer caps made of ermine fur. Moccasins were stuffed with fur or lined with an extra layer of buffalo or elk hide for added warmth, and people wrapped themselves in blankets of rabbit or groundhog fur and kept their hands warm in rabbit fur mittens.

FOOD AND THE HUNT

Salmon from the Columbia and Fraser Rivers and their tributaries was the main staple in the Plateau tribes' diet. Many of the peoples planned their lives around the annual spring running of the salmon, camping near the rivers from May to September, netting and spearing fish or catching them in weirs. The Kootenai took to the water, spearing salmon from their small, lightweight bark canoes. People enjoyed salmon eggs and some of their fresh catch, but most of the fish were smoked or sun dried. Often, berries added flavor to the drying fish. Some of the dried salmon would be crushed into a powder which would keep a long time and could be cooked as cakes or added to stews. Only the Plateau tribes knew the secret of preparing this nutritious and tasty salmon powder. Other tribes eagerly traded valuable items for this delicacy.

When the amazing rush of fish was over for the

Angelic La Moose, whose grandfather was a chief of the Flathead tribe, stands before a tepee on the Flathead Reservation in Montana in 1913, wearing a tribal costume made by her mother.

Chief Joseph of the Nez Perce fought a gallant, desperate battle with the United States Army. This photograph shows him before his surrender in 1877.

year, the tribes migrated to hunt other game such as deer, elk, and caribou. They also hunted the smaller animals such as snakes, lizards, and grasshoppers, which were often a boy's first contributions as a hunter. The women gathered the all-essential roots, vegetables, and seeds that formed a large part of the Plateau diet. Camas, one of the most important roots, provided a vital source of starch, but the tribes also devoured bitterroot, hazelnuts, and a wide variety of berries including gooseberries, strawberries, and raspberries.

The Northern Shoshone, who lived in a region where deer and elk were rare, travelled east of the Rocky Mountains each year to hunt buffalo on the Great Plains. But hunting big game was no easy matter for any of the tribes in the early days when they were afoot and had only undependable dogs to help them.

THE HORSE

As with the Plains tribes, the Plateau warriors found that the horse made warfare easier. But, as it was with the Plains tribes, war was more a matter of horse raiding and the counting of coup than serious, long-term combat. Some of the Plateau men never went to war at all. The ones who did never took scalps, but contented themselves with trophies made from locks of an enemy's hair sliced off in battle. Unlike the warriors of the Plains, none of the Plateau tribes ever formed special warrior societies or clans.

The horse probably had the greatest affect on trading. Now the Plateau tribes didn't have to depend on the Chinook canoes to bring goods to them. With horses they could trade widely on their own, going into California and the Great Plains, communicating by the sign language known throughout most of the West. They brought back everything from food to clothing, carrying shells from the Pacific to the Plains and buffalo hides from the Plains to the Pacific. Just as important as the carrying of goods was the transfer of ideas, linking the tribes through similar rituals and passing along news of the world beyond the limits of the Plateau.

Plateau women also enjoyed the benefits of the horse. Like the women of the Great Plains, they owned their own horses, and some women rose to economic importance with shrewd horse trading.

The Nez Perce were the most famous of the Plateau horsemen. The other tribes let horses breed as they would, making no attempt to cull the weak or geld undesirable stallions. The Nez Perce, on the

other hand, began a rigorous system of horse breeding, aiming for an animal that would be sturdy, swift, and attractively colored. The famous spotted horse of the Nez Perce, the Appaloosa, is still used and prized today as an all-purpose Western horse.

RITUAL AND RELIGION

Perhaps reflecting their more relaxed social order, religion among the Plateau tribes wasn't rigidly structured. Still, it was a private matter. Many of the tribes did believe in a Creator who made the world and everything on it, and who should be revered. Some also believed in an evil opposite, who must never receive prayers. All the Plateau peoples believed in Coyote, the immortal trickster and hero in one, who, they said, had been sent down to Earth to keep things moving and make life easier for people by introducing them to salmon and teaching them to hunt. According to some tales, Coyote even set the seasons to turning properly.

A child of the Plateau tribes was initiated into ritual even before birth. A pregnant woman avoided anything that might upset her. She bathed regularly in cold water, prayed daily, and ate only the flesh of birds and fish. Her husband, too, had to bathe regularly and offer his prayers for a healthy child.

Once a Plateau boy or girl reached puberty, a new set of rituals began, which included daily bathing and prayers for strength and health. Like the Plains peoples, the tribes of the Plateau believed that Vision Quests were necessary to gain spirit guardians. Both boys and girls went on such quests.

Sometimes a child might receive so overwhelmingly powerful a vision that he or she might become a shaman as a result. Shamans among the Plateau tribes weren't sorcerers to be feared, but healers attuned to the spirit and animal world. The tribe would turn to the shaman if the buffalo couldn't be found, so that the shaman might dream and locate the herd for the hunters. In addition to the healing work of the shaman, women of the Flathead and Kootenai tribes formed a mystic society known as the Crazy Owl Society, whose purpose was to ward off disease.

The Plateau tribes were respectful of the spirits around them. A hunter prayed for game, but never forgot to offer thanks to his prey after a kill, since the animal's spirit lingered after death to be sure that its bones were treated with respect. The

Wolf Necklace, a chief of the Paloos, poses proudly for his picture in 1890, wearing shell and bead jewelry.

Plateau tribes greeted the berry season with respect, too. A large dance tepee would be erected ceremonially. Within it, at the back of the tepee, the tribe would build an altar and place the skull of a grizzly bear on it. Then they would dance the Grizzly Dance, and sing to the powerful Bear Spirit in thanksgiving. Like the Pacific Coast peoples, the Plateau tribes practiced a ritual to welcome the salmon, which was a solemn event including prayer and silent feasting.

A form of the Sun Dance was brought into the Plateau region along with trading goods. Unlike the Plains versions, though, the Plateau Sun Dance involved no self-torture. Instead, a Sun Dance chief would be chosen from among the tribe, which was a great honor. It was the duty of the Sun Dance chief and his helpers to secretly make and dress the Sun Dance doll that represented the powers behind the dance. The young men who chose to danced before the Sun Doll for a full day or night, and any who felt the need might join in. When the dance was completed, the Sun Dance doll was taken away and hidden from the tribe.

A woman of the Plateau tribes rides her mount in traditional costume at a Pendleton, Oregon, Pow Wow. Women of the Plateau and Plains tribes often owned their own horse herds, and had reputations as shrewd horse traders.

THE COMING OF THE WHITE MAN

First came a Yankee sea captain, Robert Gray, who in 1792 sailed up the Columbia River—named by him after his ship—into what would later become the Oregon Territory. Then the Lewis and Clark Expedition of 1804 to 1806 marked the first true warning of major changes to come to the Plateau tribes, as the government of the young United States began to realize the region's economic potential. The years immediately following the expedition saw an influx of whites and a sudden surge in trade between the newcomers and the Plateau tribes. Tragically, the white traders brought their diseases with them, against which the Plateau tribes had no resistance. Between 1829 and 1832, diseases such as smallpox nearly exterminated the entire Chinook people.

A decade later, the white traders were replaced by a wave of settlers, heading by the thousands towards the rich land of Oregon over the newly opened Oregon Trail. As towns sprang up and expansion continued, Plateau tribal lands were imperiled, then, acre by acre, lost through treacherous treaties. The peoples of the Plateau fought back in several bloody battles, but they were outnumbered and confronted too often by better-armed troops of United States soldiers.

Any hope of success the Plateau tribes might have had was further complicated by the presence of well-meaning missionaries who, by the middle of the nineteenth century, had Christianized half of the Nez Perce, permanently dividing the tribe. The Christianized Nez Perce signed a treaty ceding away their tribal lands. The rest of the Nez Perce rejected the treaty. Led by the heroic Chief Joseph, they fought bravely, carrying on a running battle with the United States cavalry northward for long, weary miles. In 1877, they were trapped by the soldiers only thirty miles from Canadian sanctuary, and forced, as were most of the Plateau tribes, onto reservations.

While some of the descendants of the Plateau tribes have been "mainstreamed" into the wider scale of American life, others still live on those reservations, which are spread throughout Oregon, Idaho, and Montana. After successful lawsuits during the second half of this century, some of the tribes have been reimbursed, at least in part, for the lands taken from them. In addition, tribal councils in the three states are working to attract new industries and bring new jobs into the area. The Nez Perce continue to breed the Appaloosa. Like other tribes, they have taken up commercial ranching, and are building recreational facilities to bring in the tourist dollar.

THE EASTERN WOODLANDS, NORTH AND SOUTH

THE LANDS OF THE NORTHERN WOODLANDS AND GREAT LAKES

When the first Native Americans settled in the northern woodlands during the first millennium B.C., the forest was so thick the sunlight barely filtered through the ceiling of leaves. The vast region stretching from the Atlantic Ocean to the Mississippi River, from the upper shores of Lake Superior to the northern border of what is now Tennessee, was home to a wide variety of animal and plant life: deer, beaver, rabbit, and birds in the forest, waterfowl along the rivers and lakes. A mixture of hard and softwoods in the forest along with berry bushes provided a rich harvest of fruit and nuts. The sweep of forest was broken only by lakes and rivers teeming with fish. While the winters could be bitter, the climate was basically a

In the Architect of the Capitol series, Eastern Woodlands men gather to discuss tribal policy in this 1868 painting by Seth Eastman, Indian Council.

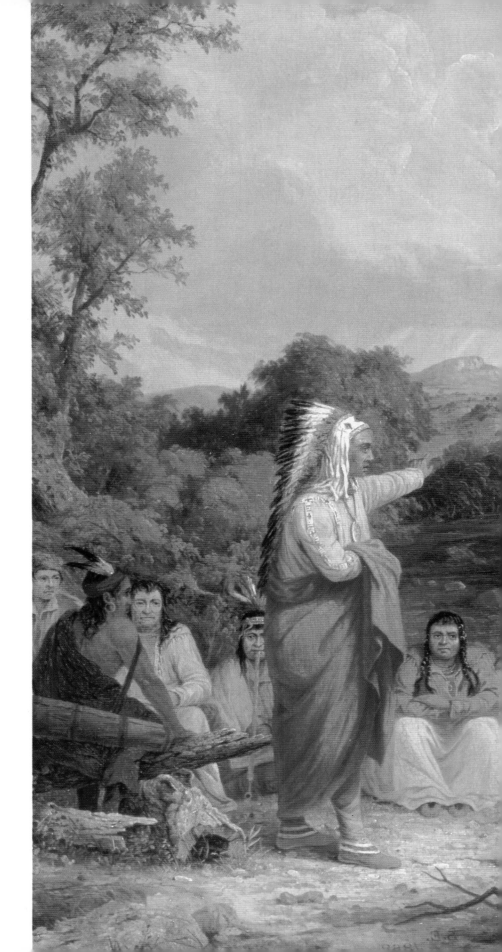

Living at the edge of the eastern woodlands, the Ojibwa built bark canoes, and covered the wooden framework of their lodges with bark or hides.

temperate one, with enough rainfall to keep the woodland lush and healthy. This was a green, fruitful world, and the many tribes who settled in it could support themselves by hunting and fishing, or farming the rich soil.

THE PEOPLE OF THE NORTHERN WOODLANDS

Over forty different tribes inhabited the region. The Huron, the Mohawk, and the ill-fated Mahicans romanticized by James Fenimore Cooper, called the Woodlands home. We remember the lands of other tribes with the names of places such as Narragensett, Penobscot, and Tuscarora.

At the western edge of the Woodlands, in what is now Wisconsin, the Winnebago tribes were related to some of the Dakotas of the Great Plains and spoke Siouan. Most of the other Woodland tribes were related through language and culture, speaking some dialect of the widespread Native American language known as Algonquian, which has added "moose," "moccasin," and "tomahawk" to our own language.

SOCIETY

Most of the Woodlands tribes were relatively small, some well under a thousand people. The larger tribes were divided into smaller bands, linked by kinship ties. Among such people as the Huron, these bands lived side by side, speaking a common language. Among other tribes, the bands scattered widely so that people from two different bands might speak two different dialects. Most of the Woodlands tribes were matrilineal, counting descent through the mother's family, and matrilocal, meaning that a bridegroom left his family and moved in with his wife's family. Each tribe was divided up into clans; members of each clan were related, no matter how distantly, by descent from a common female ancestor.

Women had a good deal of social and political power among the tribes. For example, though the tribal chiefs were always male, a new chief must always be nominated by the Clan Mother, the eldest or wisest woman in the tribe. The candidate would then be elected or rejected by the rest of the tribe. His first duty was to uphold the tribal peace and support the law with the aid of warriors who served as the village police force. The Clan Mother advised him in all these areas.

THE IROQUOIS CONFEDERACY

Later in the tribes' history, just before whites settled in the northeast, the formation of the Iroquois Confederacy proved one notable exception to the Woodlands norm of fortified, separate villages. The land between Lake Erie and the Hudson River Valley, including most of upper New York State, was the territory of five different nations united under the Iroquois Confederacy.

Sometimes called the League of the Iroquois, the powerful Iroquois Confederacy united the Mohawk, Oneida, Onondaga, Cayuga, and Seneca. As one federation, it was the major enemy of the Algonquian tribes and the independent Huron. During the early 1500s, the Five Nations of the Confederacy were constantly at war with each other, even though they were kin. But then a man of peace, a Huron named Deganawidah, together with his disciple, Hiawatha (not the hero of Longfellow's famous poem) travelled among the tribes, promoting his vision of a mighty "tree of peace" whose roots were the Five Nations. The Confederacy that was formed as a result of his teachings was perhaps the New World's first democracy, complete with an oral constitution, and a governing council composed of fifty chiefs, all equal in the eyes of Iroquois law. The Iroquois Confederacy created a lasting peace between the five tribes. When the Tuscarora were displaced by European settlers in the eighteenth century in the Carolinas, the Confederacy became six. In the late eighteenth century, their sophisticated government impressed such great thinkers as Benjamin Franklin, who wanted to know why fledgling America couldn't be as well organized.

HOMES AND VILLAGES

Most of the peoples of the northern Woodlands lived in homes called longhouses, a literal description of their long and narrow shape. Wooden poles tied together provided the framework, which was then covered with sheets of bark. Each had doors at the front and back and a rounded roof with smoke holes at intervals down its length. Sometimes the outer walls were painted in intricate red and black designs. Five or six families, related through blood or marriage, shared each longhouse. Whenever a new marriage meant that more room was needed within a longhouse, it was a relatively simple matter for the families to remove one end of the house, add on as many poles as necessary to make it longer, cover them with bark, and replace the house end.

Porches at both ends held such foods as corn stored in birchbark containers. Within a longhouse, families hung their belongings on pegs from central posts, which helped support the roof. Furniture was simple. Sleeping platforms lined the walls, and served as benches when people were awake, and a second tier of platforms higher up provided yet more storage space. Individual family cooking fires, which burned in a row down the center of the house, provided heat and light. Some covered the bare earthen floor of their homes with sheets of bark or mats woven from bark or corn husks. Mats also made good coverings for the open doorways and, if desired, could serve as dividers between family sections along the length of the house.

There were, of course, regional variations. Some of the more northern Woodlands tribes, such as the Chippewa and Ottawa, built smaller, dome-shaped bark-covered wigwams instead of longhouses.

Those Woodland tribes not related by blood or clan ties were, like the Hurons and the Five Nations, often bitter enemies. Their villages, which consisted of a gathering of longhouses laid out in an orderly crosshatching of "streets," were walled in by protective wooden palisades made of sharpened stakes. Rocks for repelling invaders and water to

Constructed of wooden poles covered with bark, a typical Iroquois longhouse was home to several families, all of them related through their mothers' bloodlines. Each family slept on raised platforms screened by woven mats. Central cooking fires that ran the length of the house provided heat and light.

This cornhusk mask, like those of the Iroquois False Face societies, was a sacred object, reflecting the powers of the Earth, and was always treated with great respect.

of wooden strips laced tightly together and carried large shields of cedar bark.

The point of a raid was to get into an enemy village and do as much quick damage and gain as much personal honor through the killing of a foe as possible before leaving. Siouan tribes like the Winnebago rated the counting of coups highly, but scalp taking was common among the other Woodlands peoples.

The raiders' successful return culminated in a feast and a Scalp Dance, during which the enemy scalps were mounted on poles and displayed to all the people. The women decided the fate of prisoners, who were paraded before them, and kept the scalps from the raid for safekeeping. If a particular captive were fortunate, he might be adopted into the tribe to replace a deceased member. Otherwise, his death would be slow and painful, his only hope to die bravely so that his name might be remembered with honor.

HUNTING AND FARMING

What the Woodlands peoples ate, and how they got their food, depended, of course, on their surroundings. Tribes such as the Delaware and Powhatan, who lived on the fertile coastal plains in a relatively mild climate, had easy access to the rich fishing of the then untapped Atlantic shore. Once the trees lining the coast were cleared from the fertile soil, the tribes also raised such crops as corn, using seaweed and dead fish to make nitrogen-rich fertilizer. The Montauk tribe of New York's Long Island had another seaside asset: clam beds untainted by any touch of pollution. But most of the inland peoples depended as much on agriculture for their food as on any fish or game their hunters could catch.

The highly valued labor of farming was considered women's work by most of the Woodlands tribes. First the men cleared the fields, which

The Woodlands tribes living near the Great Lakes grew wild rice, which was a staple part of their diets. Tribes like the Ojibwa still take part in rice harvests.

put out any fires those invaders might set were stored in the watchtowers and ramparts along the walls.

WAR

A war raid started with the choosing of a war chief, a warrior skilled in battle who had been granted a dream or vision of success. Those who wished to join him on the raid would show their acceptance of him by smoking a sacred pipe of tobacco, then gathering at his longhouse for a feast and a planning session. The war bundle, which contained objects sacred to individual warriors, was honored and prepared for carrying on the upcoming raid.

Warriors armed themselves with bows and arrows or clubs. Though raiders often couldn't afford to slow themselves down with so much extra weight, they sometimes wore arrow-resistant armor

The Iroquois easily added space to the longhouse as each daughter brought her new husband home to live with the clan. They removed the rear wall of the longhouse, added extra poles covered with bark, and replaced the already assembled rear wall.

Some Northeast Woodlands tribes depended on agriculture as much as hunting. Women of the Huron tribe hoed the land and planted precious corn seed. They often fertilized their fields with dead fish.

The Mohawks, a powerful tribe member of the Iroquois Confederacy, now occupy a large reservation in New York State and Ontario. This Mohawk man wears an elaborate festival costume.

81

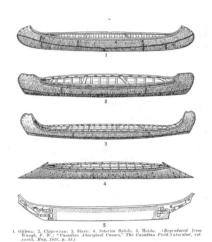

Tribes in different areas developed their own canoe designs to suit water conditions. At the top, the relatively light-weight eastern Woodlands bark canoes of the Ojibwa and Chippewa were ideal for rivers and streams. At the bottom, the heavier Pacific Northwest Haida canoe made of solid wood braved the open ocean.

Adam Fortunate Eagle, a Chippewa man from the Fallon Indian Reservation in Nevada, smokes a ritual pipe. Since pipe smoking among the tribes is considered a sacred activity, taking a photograph of any Native American smoking his pipe can only be done with his permission.

meant cutting back trees using stone-blade axes and fire to burn back the undergrowth. Then the women set to work breaking up the soil with their wooden picks and hoes. They planted such crops as the all-important corn, a staple part of tribal diet, as well as beans and squash. Sunflowers were grown also for their seeds and oil. Women also gathered wild plants and nuts from the surrounding forest, including mushrooms, fruit, and acorns. Those peoples, like the Chippewa and Menominee, who lived within easy access of the Great Lakes, harvested wild rice. In fact, the very name Menominee (or Menominiwok) means "Wild Rice Men." Some tribes, such as the Cayuga, who depended on hunting and gathering for most of their food, camped by sugar maple groves each spring so that they could add maple sugar to their diets.

Although sometimes a man of the Woodlands tribes might go fishing alone along one of the many streams, fishing expeditions to the Great Lakes or one of their tributaries were communal affairs, sometimes lasting as long as a month. The fishermen built temporary wood and bark houses for themselves in which to live before returning to the village with their catch of whitefish, trout, or sturgeon. The men fished with nets or weirs and killed them with bone-tipped fish spears.

Hunting was a communal effort, too. The Woodlands tribes hunted game birds including geese, heron, and turkey, and animals such as beaver and bear, but their main goal was deer. The whitetail deer was as important to the survival of the Woodlands culture as the buffalo was to that of the Plains tribes. Its meat fed the people, while its hide provided clothing and sinews made the thread to sew that clothing together. Deer bones were turned into awls and needles, amulets and jewelry, and the bright whitetail hair was used in ritual headdresses. The antlers made excellent digging tools, and were an integral part of a chief's symbolic crown. Not even the hoofs of a deer were wasted; filled with pebbles, they became rattles for the people's dances.

Something as vital as a deer hunt wasn't undertaken lightly. Before such a hunt, a man would pray to his guardian spirits for help, fasting or deliberately shedding his own blood to show his genuine need. Then he would join the other hunters, who had scouted out a concentration of deer, or had been given a herd's location through the tribal shaman's visions. The deer were hunted in drives that forced the frightened animals in a chosen direction, where they could be easily killed. Some

tribes, like the Huron, used hunting dogs to help them. The Huron became particularly attached to their dogs, giving them pet names and allowing them into the longhouses.

No wise Woodlands hunter ever forgot to be respectful of the spirits of the animals he'd slain, thanking them for giving up their lives and treating their bodies with honor.

CLOTHING AND TOOLS

Before Europeans brought wool and cloth into the region, deer provided the Woodlands tribes with most of their clothing, though some of the more northern peoples used moosehide as well. Women designed and made the clothing, and while style and quality varied from tribe to tribe, the fashion basics remained the same. Men generally wore a breechcloth, leggings, and buckskin moccasins, frequently ornamented with paint or dyed porcupine quills. A woman would add a sleeveless overdress, though in the hotter summers of the southern Woodlands, she might wear little more than a skirt. Her clothing, too, would be decorated. In the winter, heavier moccasins and leggings were necessary. If the snow was particularly heavy, people travelled about on snowshoes crafted from woven bark and branches.

Hairstyles among the Woodland tribes varied wildly, particularly among the men, who might sport anything from the traditional "Mohawk" to a scalp shaven and painted on one side of the head. Women's hair was long, kept in a single plait or double braids down the back.

Before they had access to silver—which came into the region with the traders and became very popular for bracelets and pendants—Woodlands people wore shell bracelets, necklaces, and earrings. Shell plaques might hang at women's waists or dangle from their braids. At a festival, a woman in all her shell finery might wear as much as twelve pounds of beads. Feathers were also used in jewelry, and men sometimes wore ruffs of down as well. Headbands of snakeskin or eel skin were popular, too, and people frequently painted themselves in red and black designs for festive or religious occasions.

The making of wampum was another less frivolous use for shell beads. The wampum, strings and strips of beads, were symbols of the pledged word. Granted as a sign of honor to a worthy man, they were exchanged in marriage contracts or political agreements, preserving the terms of treaty between tribes or nations. Both a sacred artifact and a

Local craftsmen made knives, arrowheads, and other tools out of chert, or North American flint, wood, animal bones, and antlers. Animal sinews bound blades to hilts or spears to shafts.

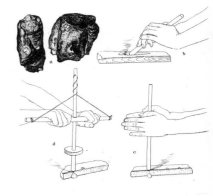

Native Americans produced fire by striking two flinty rocks together to create sparks, which then ignited carefully mounded tinder. Various kinds of friction drills also produced enough heat to light the tinder.

means of conveying important messages, wampum is still used by the Iroquois today.

In addition to the reed- or corn-leaf mats used for floors and door coverings, the Woodlands peoples also wove baskets of reeds or sewed pieces of birchbark together to make containers. Pottery vessels, large and strictly utilitarian, were also used in some regions. Clay was also important for the manufacture of elegant pipes, finely polished and often complete with detailed effigy figures. Though some of the plain pipes were used purely for pleasure, most were an aspect of religious life. Twine from Indian hemp was the basic material for fish nets, and some tribes, such as the Huron, also wove it into scarves and bracelets.

The members of the Iroquois Confederacy also were skillful woodcarvers, using chert blades to create elegant ceremonial bowls and ladles, and

Unami/Delaware moccasins dating from the late eighteenth century show classic eastern Woodlands style. Each has been cut from a single piece of deerskin and decorated with porcupine quills and tin bangles with red-dyed deer hair.

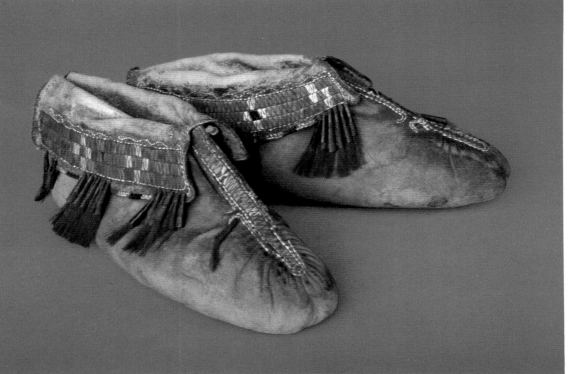

intricately ornamented cradle boards. Larger projects, such as cutting down trees, required axes and chisels of harder, less brittle diorite or granite. Chert or bone was used in arrowheads and spear points, and women sewed with needles and awls worked from deer bones.

The canoe was one of the most important means of transportation for the Woodlands people. While coastal tribes usually preferred to simply shape and hollow out a tree with adzes and hot rocks, the inland tribes built the famous birchbark canoe, useful on the many streams, rivers, and lakes. Birchbark canoes came in a variety of sizes, from an easily portable one-man model to boats large enough to hold a six-man crew. All the canoes showed the same basic design: wooden ribs, bent into shape after being soaked in hot water to soften them, were covered with thick sheets of bark, usually from white birch, which were sewn into place. White pine pitch was then heated and used to coat and seal all the seams, making a lightweight, waterproof craft.

An Ojibwa Chief, *by George Catlin, c. 1843; National Gallery of Art, Washington; Paul Mellon Collection.*
Although this Ojibwa chief's name is lost to us, his pride and the elegance of his clothing point out the importance of his rank.

SOCIAL LIFE

The Woodlands tribes "took care of their own," chipping in to help a clan member in distress, replacing lost or destroyed goods, or rebuilding a burned-out house. People to whom stinginess was a crime, eagerly welcomed guests and public feasts were common. Meals included everything from roasted meat, corn, and squash to corn soup, fish stew, and unleavened bread flavored with dried fruit or deer fat.

Although there were certain taboos, primarily the one forbidding two members of the same clan to wed, courtship and marriage among the Woodlands tribes wasn't quite a formalized affair. Properly, a boy's family arranged the whole matter of finding him a suitable bride. While they did suggest proper mates, the two young people often did their own choosing. A boy would ask the girl's parents for their consent. If they said yes, he would then offer the girl of his choice a present. After she accepted it, and him, the young people would live together in

a brief trial marriage. If the girl decided things were going well, there would then be a more formal wedding. Later, either partner could initiate divorce if necessary.

The Woodlands tribes also had taboos that a pregnant woman must observe. If she looked at deformed animals, her unborn child might suffer. Eating turtle or rabbit meat might make the child move awkwardly. In some tribes, the actual birth took place in a hut ritually erected for the purpose. Immediately after birth, a baby was fastened into a cradle board cushioned with soft, absorbent moss,

which served as a diaper that could be changed as often as necessary. Small toys and charms hung from the hood of the cradle board to entertain the baby.

Children were cherished by the Woodlands tribes. Girl babies were especially welcome, both because they continued the matrilineal line of the clan's descent and as potential childbearers themselves. Among the Iroquois nations, the Clan Mother usually named the tribe's babies, but other Woodlands tribes hired professional namers, who acted more or less as godparents. Later, the grow-ing young man or woman would receive an adult name through deeds or visions.

Boys and girls received the start of their adult training at an early age. A girl learned the rudi-ments of farming, weaving, and other tasks, while a boy learned the skills of a hunter and warrior. At puberty, Woodlands boys often underwent a Vision Quest similar to those undertaken by boys of the Great Plains tribes. A girl undergoing her first menstruation would stay apart from her tribe in a special hut, where she prayed for health and fruitfulness. Upon her return to her family, a feast would be held in her honor.

Ritual also surrounded the end of one's life on Earth. When a member of the family died, he or she was dressed in his or her finest clothing and orna-ments. The body was taken out through the west-ern wall of the house, in the direction of the land of the dead. Some of the tribes buried their dead directly in the ground, with ceremonies depending on the deceased person's clan and rank. The Huron first interred their dead in coffins raised on poles. After ten to twelve years, the bones were taken down and buried in a communal pit, and a great Feast of the Dead was held in the honor of all those who had died.

RELIGION

The world of the Woodlands tribes teemed with powerful spirits, present in Earth, forest, and sky. Some of them were benign, such as a man's own guardian spirit, to be honored and propitiated. Others, like the winter stalker of the more northern tribes, the Wendigo, were feared.

The tribes of the Iroquois Confederacy believed that humanity began when Sky-Woman, impreg-nated by the Earth Holder, fell to Earth, where she gave birth to Great Spirit and Evil Spirit. After her death, Great Spirit turned her head into the sun and her body into the moon and stars, then went on

A Winnebago hoop dancer performs his complicated dance pattern.

to create life on Earth. Her brother, Evil Spirit, was banished to the Netherworld, but continues to try to harm Great Spirit's creations. The Iroquois tried to please the spirits of the natural world.

Perhaps the most familiar religious organization to outsiders is the False Face Society, which was a healing society whose members wore sacred masks representing the mercurial and sometimes dangerous forces that could be used for curing the sick. So sacred and powerful are these masks that one could never be left face up, nor should one be placed on public display.

Several ceremonies, celebrated with ritual dancing and feasting, made up the Woodlands year, far too many to be listed here. The Green Corn

Drawn between 1833 and 1834, this double portrait of Massica, a Sauk warrior, and Wakusakke, a warrior of the Fox tribe, shows off their distinctive hairstyles and face paint.

Festival, held in late summer, was a particularly important rite of thanksgiving which celebrated the gift of corn. The Iroquois Ceremonial of Midwinter was perhaps even more important. A solstice celebration taking place for a week, it brought in the New Year through days of solemn rituals and dancing. The Midwinter festival included a form of trick-or-treating in which groups of young people, led by an old woman, roamed the village, dancing and singing in exchange for presents.

There were four types of highly respected shaman: those who could affect the weather, those who could predict the future, those who were healers, and those who could find lost objects. Woodlands shamans were usually men, though women sometimes became diviners.

A Delaware man wears traditional dance regalia, from face paint to fringed leggings.

THE COMING OF THE EUROPEANS

The first Europeans to arrive in the New World early in the seventeenth century came as traders. The French eventually settled what would become Quebec, while the English and some of the Dutch populated the lands further south. At first, relations with the tribes were peaceful. The Europeans exchanged metal goods for the tribes' knowledge of the land. But the peace couldn't last. The Iroquois Confederacy used its newly gained European firearms to nearly wipe out the enemy Huron in 1649, making itself the dominant Woodlands force for nearly half a century. Meanwhile, the number of European settlers steadily increased, as did their demand for more land.

In Virginia, the local tribes had already fought for and lost their home to the English. The pattern would repeat itself further north. The tribes became involved in European wars on Native American soil. First, the Iroquois Confederacy fought with the British against France. Then the American Revolutionary War broke out between the colonies and England. The Iroquois, allies of the English, suffered a defeat at American hands that destroyed them as a power. Soon the other tribes would face defeat of a different sort as they, like the southern tribes, were forced from their lands. In 1832, the Fox and Sauk tribes mounted one last battle under the leadership of the warrior Black Hawk. Their loss marked the end of tribal control of their homeland.

Today, the descendants of the Woodlands tribes are scattered throughout the United States and Canada, some on the reservations on which they were forcibly resettled, others in the "mainstream." Perhaps the most successful are those Iroquois who remained in New York State and now own territory in northern New York and southern Ontario. The Seneca, in particular, have been awarded $15 million in settlement for their seized land and for development projects, and have a constitutional government incorporated under New York State; they also own property in the town of Salamanca. The Mohawk have perhaps become the best known of the Nations to outsiders, since some of their men have become famous as high-rise steel construction workers who helped build such New York landmarks as the Empire State Building.

THE PEOPLE

Before white settlers pushed them off the land, anywhere from one to two million Native American peoples lived in the northeast Woodlands. A wide variety of tribes spoke as many different languages. Though language and geography separated them, southern tribes shared a number of beliefs and customs. In fact, when the tribes broke up or were destroyed with the arrival of the Europeans, members from one tribe could fit into another tribe without too much difficulty.

Some of the better known tribes of the southeast Woodlands include the Chickasaw, Cherokee, Creek, Choctaw, Natchez, Apalachee, and Timuaca. During the eighteenth century, members of the Creek, Oconee, Yamanase, and even runaway black slaves, banded together to create the Seminole of Florida.

HOME AND THE VILLAGE

Hunters and farmers, most southeastern Woodlands people led a settled, rather than nomadic, way of life. Full-time farmers needed to tend their crops. Wooden palisades as high as sixteen feet protected their villages. Sometimes a mixture of mud and grass covered the palisades for additional strength. Within the palisade, homes clustered around a central council house.

Each group of homes included a family's lightweight summer shelter, which was designed to catch every possible breeze, and the more heavily insulated winter house, which had no windows and only one low doorway. Though life was communal, a family might also own storage sheds, a granary, and a household garden. Wooden poles provided a rectangular or round frame, protected with woven cane walls covered with clay and grass, and topped with a roof of woven saplings with bark shingles.

Within each family's house there were wooden sleeping platforms covered with furs or woven cane mats. Green or yellow cane woven baskets, frequently decorated with red and black dyed designs, held family necessities. In the winter house, a central fire constantly burned for warmth as well as cooking. The smoke escaped only through a hole in the roof, so the house was usually smokey as well as warm.

As tall as twenty-five feet, the central council house met certain ritual requirements—its outer wall must contain seven pillars, representing the mystical seven directions, and the seats of the highest members of the tribe must be whitened

A Miccosukee man demonstrates the fine art of alligator wrestling.

THE LANDS OF THE SOUTHEAST WOODLANDS

Stretching from the Gulf of Mexico to what is now lower Mississippi, Ohio, Kentucky, and Virginia, from the Atlantic coastal marshes to the Mississippi River, the southeast is blessed with fertile soil, mild winters, and abundant rainfall. Native Americans first settled this region sometime after the first millennium B.C. They entered a paradise of lush forested land full of game and edible plants, with rivers teeming with fish.

Many of the Native American tribes used feathers in their ceremonial outfits, and the Choctaw were no exception, as this colorful headdress reveals. Such feathers often had a symbolic or religious meaning, usually involving the wearer's worth and honor.

with clay to signify purity and holiness. People gathered here for meetings, ceremonies, or dancing. It also provided shelter for the village poor and homeless. Village life also centered around a game field, which doubled as an open-air museum of the tribe's military victories.

There were, of course, regional variations. For example, the Seminole lived in a hot, swampy environment and built their thatch-roofed, open-sided houses on stilts above the damp ground to help keep them dry.

SOCIAL LIFE

The southern tribes were, almost without exception, matrilineal, counting descent through the mother's side of the family. As a result, a child was thought of as belonging to the mother, with the

A member of the Miccosukee tribe of Florida wears many colorful bead necklaces.

mother's brother taking over the role of a male parent. The tribes also divided themselves into all-important clans: A person's first loyalty was to the clan and the tribe second.

Though the Clan Mothers also held village authority, a council made up of those who had become famous in wartime or peaceful activities such as healing ruled the village. The council met to discuss matters of concern to everyone. Any villager could attend and speak at the meetings. Each could vote on major decisions, and the majority ruled.

Social life revolved around one's clan. Marriage between clan members was forbidden. If two youngsters of different clans wanted to marry, the proper etiquette insisted that the young man first ask his mother's sister for help. She, in turn, would approach the young woman's maternal aunt. If both women approved, the boy could go ahead and ask the girl for her hand.

Pregnancy and birth were also ritualized. A pregnant woman ate certain foods to guarantee the baby's health. Lingering in doorways might make the baby linger in the womb. Her diet was salt-free to ensure an easy birth.

White's hunger for land drove most of the Cherokee tribes from their eastern Woodlands homes to Oklahoma in what is called the Trail of Tears in 1838. Today, a Cherokee enclave remains in North Carolina.

A girl was considered a woman at the time of her first menstruation, but a boy remained a boy until the day he took part in a battle and proved his manhood by wounding or killing an enemy. To mark his new status, he would be awarded an adult name and, if he had performed an outstanding feat, a war title as well. Titles were awarded during a lengthy ceremony that included three days of ritual bathing, dancing, and feasting, and ordeals of sleeplessness to demonstrate the honored warrior's worth.

RELIGION

Religion was closely related to government among the southern tribes. A council member was dedicated in childhood, and underwent much of the same training of a young shaman or medicine man. A medicine man was an honored member of the tribe. In addition to serving as a priest, he was often a skilled healer with a wide range of effective herbal medicines, many of which are being studied by modern science.

The tribes of the south believed in the spirits just as any other Native American tribe. They felt that woodland spirits hid among the trees. They also believed in a supreme deity, a three-fold god so sacred the name was not spoken aloud. The sun and the moon protected the people and gave them fire. In addition, there were other important supernatural beings, such as those who symbolized the four directions: North or Defeat, West or Death, South or Peace, and East or Power in War.

Some tribes, such as the Cherokee, placed special significance on the sacred number seven. There were seven ritual ceremonies, six taking place every year, the seventh to be performed once every seven years. Most revolved around the seasons, celebrating the first new moon of spring, the ripening of the new corn crop, or the season's harvest.

All the tribes celebrated Busk, the autumn harvest festival, as their most sacred holiday. On the first day, the women cleaned and swept the family homes while the men took care of the council houses. All fires, including the sacred fires burning in the council house, were extinguished. On the second and third days the people fasted. On the fourth day, they held a great feast and the tribe's shaman lit a ceremonial fire from which all the family fires could be relit. The shaman roasted ears of corn in the ceremonial fire. The new year had begun.

WAR

There were often feuds between the various clans. And often these feuds would spill out from one village to engulf two tribes in genuine warfare. A declaration of war wasn't made in haste; first the tribal council would meet and debate the issue. A woman, known as Honored Woman or War Woman, represented the female vote in Cherokee war councils. If the council could find no peaceful solution, the red-painted war club would be displayed in the village, and a red flag of battle flown. The elected war leader would rouse his warriors, and the women would sing fierce war songs. The warriors spent three days preparing themselves by ritual purification and fasting, then armed themselves with whatever weapons each warrior preferred, from bows and arrows to slings or lances, painted themselves in the war colors of red and black, and set off into the field. Their leader carried a medicine bundle full of powerful charms.

Surprise was the warriors' favorite tactic; if a band was discovered before it could attack, it might very well retreat without striking a blow. Unlike the swift raids of the Plains tribes, where the primary objective was the counting of coup, the southeast battles were fierce and deadly, often resulting in the taking of scalps or even the killing of all the enemy. The fate of any enemies unlucky enough to be taken captive rested in the hands of the women. A man might be adopted into the village, or enslaved, but if his luck was particularly bad, he would be condemned to death by torture. Then his only hope was to die as bravely as possible so that he would be remembered with honor.

HUNTING AND FARMING

As with the tribes of the northern Woodlands, in the south men hunted and fished, and the women tended the fields. When a village needed a new field, the men would clear the land, then turn the rest of the work over to the women, who planted such crops as corn, beans, squash, and pumpkins. They were skillful farmers, growing corn and beans together so that the cornstalks would provide support for the clinging beanstalks. Two varieties of corn were planted, one quick to mature, one growing more slowly, so that ears would be available throughout the summer and well into the fall. The late-maturing corn was dried and ground into meal that could be safely stored for use throughout the winter. The women also gathered wild fruits, vegetables, and forest berries.

Before the hunt, hunters prayed to the animal-spirits for forgiveness for the lives they would take. Deer, the most prized prey, provided meat, sinews for thread, hides for clothing, bones for needles and awls, and hoofs for rattles. Unlike the Great Plains tribes who hunted herds of buffalo in groups, a deer hunter stalked his solitary prey alone, sometimes disguised in a deer's hide or imitating a deer's mating call. Sometimes, though, there might be

A member of the Alabama-Coshutta dancers of east Texas performs a tribal dance in San Antonio.

93

enough deer in a portion of the forest for several hunters to work together, setting a fire to drive the animals into the open. Bear in the woods offered fur and fat rather than meat, and the varied game birds of the southern forests, in particular the wild turkey, much more wily and difficult to catch than its domestic cousin, were also prized.

A reconstructed earth lodge in Ocmulgee, Georgia, represents the style of house common among the more southern of the eastern Woodlands tribes. At the left of the photograph lies a foundation for a hearth fire.

CLOTHING

Living as they did in a warm climate, clothing was not the southern tribes' first concern. Choctaw and Creek men wore deerskin breechcloths in the summer and shirts, moccasins, and bearskin robes in the winter. Women might wear as little as deerskin skirts or aprons in the summer, and deerskin dresses, moccasins, and fur robes in the winter. Some tribes, such as the Cherokee, specialized in warm, lightweight wraps and cloaks made of turkey feathers or, for more ceremonial occasions, eagle feathers. Feathers were also worn in headdresses, and were made into fans. Tribes living in the humid swamps often wore even less than the other southern peoples; the Timuaca of Florida

This Seminole family from Florida display their colorful clothing and some of the tools of everyday life, from the baby's cradle, suspended from the roof, to the churn in the background.

needed little more than brief outfits of animal skins and trailing strands of Spanish moss. Later, the Seminole women designed colorful dresses and tunics, patterned loosely after European styles, out of scraps of imported cotton sewn together. Shell and bead necklaces and earrings were popular, and tattooing was a common form of decoration.

TRAIL TO THE WEST

The arrival of Spanish explorers in the sixteenth century radically changed the lives of the southeastern tribes, and spelled the end for many of them. The newcomers, armed with deadly firearms and steel weapons, thought nothing of destroying any who stood in their way. They also brought European diseases such as smallpox, which wiped out entire Native American villages. Before the tribes could recover from this first wave of destruction, the French and British soon started fighting over their lands. The Europeans had taken control of the lands, fighting their wars, trapping, and farming. Native Americans hunted slaves for the Europeans, who rewarded them with iron tools and rum.

By 1710, the European hunger for slaves had virtually destroyed the tribes of northern Florida. The survivors, together with runaway black slaves, joined together in the southeastern swampland to form a new people, the Seminole. Though most Seminole were exiled by the new United States government, others held out for years in the Florida swamps, waging guerrilla warfare until at last they won; their descendants still occupy their lands, and have successfully sued the United States government for restitution and lands.

Other tribes weren't so fortunate. As the new American nation grew, it demanded more and more land to produce cotton. Soon the state governments insisted on their removal: They were already outnumbered by the white settlers. The tribes' people were uncivilized "heathens," not worthy of the land they held. Even though the Cherokee, Choctaw, Chickasaw, Creek, and Seminole had long since incorporated Christianity into religious ritual, the Five Civilized Tribes had no choice. In 1830, the government forcibly relocated the Choctaw to Oklahoma on a harsh winter march that saw more than a quarter of the unwilling emigrants succumbing to hunger or sheer exhaustion.

Between 1834 and 1838, the Creek, Cherokees, and Chickasaws followed them in what was to become known as the Trail of Tears. Exiled to Oklahoma, the Creek took the last Native spirit from the lands southeast of the Mississippi. America pushed west to Texas and the Great Plains.

But a small remnant of the Cherokee nation did, like the Seminole, manage to hold onto at least part of its land by obtaining United States citizenship, which exempted them from being ousted. (However, most Native Americans were not considered citizens until an act of Congress in 1924.) Today, descendants of those Cherokee occupy legally purchased reservation lands in North Carolina. They continue to use the written language devised by the brilliant Sequoyah in the early nineteenth century, and keep the customs of their ancestors.

Oseola, a chief of the Seminole tribes of Florida, sat for this portrait by George Catlin in 1837.

A Little Osage chief of 1807 displays a hairstyle popular among his Florida tribes.

Some eastern Woodlands tribes were expert fishermen. Artist John White portrayed South Carolina fishermen in 1585 going after their prey with spears, nets, and traps.

The Miccosukee use flat, open boats powered by a pole to navigate the swampy waters of Florida.

THE

SOUTHWEST

THE LAND

From the northern borders of the Grand Canyon
in Utah, east to Colorado, and south through New
Mexico and Arizona, images of the American
Southwest wash through in brilliant red and brown
desert hues. In Arizona alone, the tranquil green-
ery of Oak Creek Canyon contrasts with the myste-
rious Superstition Mountains and the black lava
beds, the *mal pais,* "bad country" beloved of snakes.
The Sonora Desert with its towering saguaro cacti
in central Arizona is a far cry from the pink and
blue sands stretching throughout the Painted
Desert in northern Arizona. In Colorado, the Grand
Canyon records centuries past in its layers of rock.

The hard land, scorched by the heat and cooled
rapidly at night absorbs little rainfall. Some rain-

*A modern-day Apache
tepee at Stone Lake on
the Jicarilla Apache
Reservation in New
Mexico is outlined
against the setting sun.*

100

A traditional Navajo home, called a hogan, made of a wooden framework covered with mud, stands before Shiprock, an extinct volcano in New Mexico.

During a Christmas celebration at San Juan Pueblo in New Mexico, a Matachine dancer practices a ritual that combines Spanish Christianity and ancient, pre-Christian ways.

Southwestern United States. Of course, others link them to the tribes arriving across the Bering Land Bridge.

The original inhabitants such as the Hohokam built such fine irrigation canals that modern Phoenix still uses them. The Anasazi, the Ancient Ones, lived in houses built into the sides of limestone cliffs, shielded from the sun and perhaps an enemy, whose name is lost in time. Their descendants, however, continue to live on the ancestral lands: the New Mexican tribes of Acoma, Jemez, Taos, and a dozen other Pueblos, and the farming tribes of Arizona, among them the Hopi, Pima, Papago, and Zuni. Many believe the Navajo and Apache are relative newcomers to the region, migrating from the Northwest Territories in Canada sometime around 1,000 A.D. Linguists point out their similarities with the Southern Athapaskan or Apachean.

SOCIETY

Although the Southwest tribes all had their own lifestyle and customs, they can be loosely divided into two major groups: herders and hunters, and farmers. The Navajo historically herded sheep and occasionally planted small gardens, and the Apache hunted and gathered food in the tradition of people not truly dependent upon crops. The rest of the Southwestern tribes mostly depended on farming for their livelihood, though each relied on different foods.

The Navajo and Apache are matrilineal and matrilocal peoples, tracing descent through the female side; a bridegroom went to live with his wife's people. Among the Apache tribes, each nuclear family had its own home amongst the members of the wife's extended family, the clan: grandparents, siblings, and the like. An elder spokeswoman or man led each clan. A tribe in turn was led by a chief or headman, who held his position by ability and charisma. He had limited power; anyone who didn't like his policies was free to walk away. When a special need arose, the tribes would gather together, forming larger bands, but since the population spread over large areas of the Southwest, they rarely needed formal organization.

Farming communities were organized much differently than hunting and gathering tribes. Though social life still centered on matrilineal clans, their dependence on agriculture necessitated different customs and rituals tied to the land. Some, such as the Zuni and Hopi, are known as the

drops never reach the desert floor, evaporating as they fall in the intense heat. When the rain does come, it comes with such intensity that the land floods. Life here adapts and flourishes in these harsh conditions. The prickly pear and other cacti produce edible fruit. The tall stalks of the saguaro provide "apartment house" accommodations in hollows created by desert birds such as the little elf owl. Snakes and lizards abound, including the large and edible iguana, together with ground squirrels, jackrabbits in the shadows of cacti and sagebrush, and peccaries, or small wild pigs.

THE PEOPLE

The people of the Southwest may have first settled there as long as 10,000 years ago at the close of the last Ice Age. Radiocarbon dating of a rock shelter on a sandstone cliff in Brazil dates to 32,000 years ago. Some scholars believe people moved north at some point to what is now the

In Canyon de Chelle, New Mexico, a Navajo family looks on as a woman works at her loom.

This young Hopi wears the intricate ceremonial outfit of a sacred Rainbow Dancer.

105

Dancers perform a buffalo ritual at the San Ildefonso Pueblo in New Mexico.

Pueblo peoples because of the adobe "apartment house" complexes, or pueblos, in which they lived year-round. Depending on the rain, seasons, and crops for their livelihood, they worked out a far more elaborate code of life than the hunting peoples.

A Pueblo clan shared a common, and distant, female ancestor. The Clan Mother, usually the oldest woman, headed each one with her brother, who was their ceremonial leader. Clan families lived closely together, and followed rigid codes of behavior, in which a man called both his own mother and her sisters "mother," and his father and uncles "father." The further back the blood ties went, the more complicated matters became; his paternal grandmother and her sisters and *their* mother and sisters were all called "grandmother."

On a wider scale, every tribal ceremony was performed by one or another secret society, which was headed by a special chief priest or priestess. Village life was usually governed by the "Chiefs' Talk," a council meeting of these religious chiefs held at the end of the Winter Solstice ceremony and headed by the chief priest of the ceremony, the Village Chief. Although the "Chiefs' Talk" didn't make the tribal laws, which were set out in their religion, it could, and did, enforce discipline if necessary.

A Pueblo might be divided by a feud. More likely, though, a branch of the tribe would split off when the Pueblo became too crowded, and start a new home elsewhere. Such a new colony would retain friendly and ceremonial relations with its "parent."

Other farming groups than the Pueblo, such as the semi-nomadic Papago and Pima tribes of southern Arizona, had a somewhat different form of society. These tribes were patrilineal, tracing their descent through the father's side of the family; a woman went to live with her husband's people. A Papago or Pima clan was made up of a male ancestor and his male descendants. There were four or five clans recognized in each village, and it was their joint right to choose a headman or chief, who acted as priest and judge. Although the Papago and Pima tribes didn't go to war happily, a village might also have a war leader, known as the "bitter man," a brave warrior priest who knew the proper spells to ensure victory. In addition, a village would almost certainly have a hunting leader, who knew the charms to guarantee enough food for the people. But it was all the village men, not only these three priest-leaders, who decided how things should be run, and who gathered every night to discuss village matters.

With drummers setting the tempo, a dancer impersonates a deer chased by hunters at San Ildefonso Pueblo in New Mexico.

With special permission from the United States Park Service, the Hopi danced for two days at Mesa Verde, an important Anasazi site in Colorado, for the first time in 500 years.

Approximately 700 years ago, a people known today only as the Anasazi, the Ancient Ones, abandoned their mesa homes in what is now New Mexico and Arizona to build adobe houses in natural limestone caves such as this one. Why did they make such a drastic change? No one knows. These are the White House Ruins at Canyon de Chelly National Monument in Arizona.

The finely shaped window and door demonstrates the skill of its architects, the Anasazi. Pueblo Bonito in New Mexico has been called one of the New World's first apartment complexes.

HOMES

Most of the Navajo people lived in hogans, round, dome-shaped houses that look something like old-fashioned beehives in profile. A framework of six or eight poles cut from pinon pine, woven together at the top leaving a smokehole, support the structure. The outside was covered with an insulating layer of mud or clay. In regions where wood was scarce, a hogan might have stone walls set in mud mortar. Some Navajo groups escaped the intense summer heat by leaving their hogans and moving into temporary, open-sided shelters made of a brush-covered roof supported by poles.

More than a shelter, the hogan was a sacred home, following the pattern established by the Holy People. A new hogan must always be consecrated. Even today, when most of the people live in "standard" houses, a family will usually have at least one hogan on its property.

Those branches of the Apache people who lived in the highlands of Arizona built wickiups, windowless homes made of woven poles and brush that

Navajo hogans are built of a wooden framework covered with mud. An interior view shows some typical turn-of-the-century family belongings on a New Mexico reservation.

111

Among the Pueblo tribes, women baked bread from ground corn. At the Taos Pueblo in New Mexico, women bake bread in their outdoor ovens during the early twentieth century.

look somewhat like the Navajo hogans in profile but lack the smooth coating of mud or clay. The Apache tribes who inhabited the desert lowlands lived in tepees like their neighbors on the Great Plains.

The Pueblo tribes originally lived on the valley floors of northern Arizona and New Mexico. When the brutal Spanish conquistadors passed through the area seeking the mythical Cities of Gold during the sixteenth century, the tribes moved, in self-defense, to the flat, easily defended tops of mesas. There they built what have been called the first New World apartment complexes, rows of adobe houses piled one atop the other, some, like those of the Hopi, three stories high, others up to five stories tall, each level connected by ladders. Many of the tribes, from the Acoma to the Zuni, still live in their ancestral homes today.

Building material in the southern Sonora Desert of Arizona, the territory of the Papago and Pima tribes, has always been scarce, but these tribes built dome-shaped homes of brush-covered poles,

Taos Pueblo in New Mexico is perhaps one of the best known of the pueblos. In this view, the stacked homes, made of adobe, inevitably remind a viewer of apartment houses. The adobe domes in the foreground are outdoor ovens.

similar in shape to the Apache wickiups, and insulated with a layer of earth. These houses had only one small door and, like the homes of the Navajo and Apache, were windowless, making them easy to protect against the extreme heat and cold of the desert climate.

An outdoor oven sits just outside a Taos Pueblo home.

113

CLOTHES AND TOOLS

When they first entered the Southwest, the Navajo dressed relatively simply. A man wore a breechcloth, leggings, and sandals woven from the yucca plant. Women's clothing also was woven from yucca fibers and included a skirt, leggings, and sandals. Both men and women covered up in woven yucca blankets during chilly desert nights. The Hopi taught the Navajo "newcomers" the art of weaving cotton and wool, and soon the woven-fiber fabrics had been replaced by these more comfortable materials. Women were quick to design attractive mantas, cloth rectangles which could be worn as shawls or tied about the waist as wraparound skirts.

When European fashions and materials reached the region, men took to wearing calico shirts and denim trousers, which, together with bandannas and cowboy boots and hats, is still one of the practical and colorful styles of choice. Women dressed—and sometimes still dress—in long, wide calico skirts and brightly colored velveteen blouses, often cinched by elegant silver belts. Sometimes they added elegantly woven fringed blankets while men preferred their blankets plain. Once the art of silversmithing reached the Navajo, they became experts, producing exquisite necklaces, earrings, and belts studded with local turquoise.

Until the introduction of cotton in the late eighteenth and early nineteenth centuries, much of the Apache's clothing was made of buckskin. A man might wear a breechcloth, a loose cotton shirt, and moccasins, topped with a cotton turban or headband. A woman's costume consisted of a two-piece buckskin dress made up of skirt and blouse, and moccasins.

Both the Navajo and the Apache peoples made good use of rawhide for ropes and bridles for their horses. Rawhide also made a good covering for saddles, which were stuffed with grass and stretched over a wooden frame. Ceremonial shields made of rawhide were stretched over a wooden frame, painted, and ornamented with feathers. Deerskin masks in the shape of deer or antelope heads, large enough to be worn by a man, helped hunters approach their prey.

Both the Navajo and Apache preferred bows and arrows as weapons, though lances and war clubs consisting of a stone encased in rawhide attached to a wooden haft, looking something like the European Medieval mace, were popular as well. Arrows generally were tipped with chert or other relatives of flint.

The people used stone slabs found in the area for grinding corn or medicines. Precious wood, carefully carved with chert or iron blades, was worked into cradle boards, digging sticks, bows and arrows, and friction drills for starting fires or working jewelry.

The Apache also used wood to make a fiddle's bow. A hollow yucca stalk served as the fiddle's sounding board, which had a single rawhide string.

Finished leather and rawhide provided emergency horseshoes, tied over an injured horse's hoofs to the "business end" of wood-handled riding crops. In addition, the Lipan Apaches, influenced by the tribes of the Plains, made their baskets out of leather, though the majority of Navajo and Apache peoples preferred woven baskets, which were frequently decorated with bands of color and leather fringes. Carrying straps were sometimes included so that a basket could be easily transported on foot or by horse, and the bottoms of these baskets were often strengthened with rawhide. Water carrying vessels were covered with pitch to keep them waterproof.

Perhaps the most famous woven items of the Navajo are the colorful woolen blankets woven by their women. Although the earliest blankets made in the early nineteenth century bore the simplest of stripes, by the end of that century weavers were tapping into the white market with intricate, elegant geometrics, and even pictorial rugs showing birds and animals, and experimenting with new materials, such as silk and European flannels.

Though some of the Pueblo peoples did wear

The Navajo, like many of the Pueblo peoples, have been master silversmiths for over 100 years. In 1880, a Navajo silversmith posed with his tools and some examples of his art.

Many of the Pueblo tribes excel in pottery making. Potters at Santa Clara Pueblo in New Mexico display their craft in 1916.

Sunlight streams down into the ruins of an ancient Anasazi kiva in southern Utah. Like the modern Pueblo tribes, each band of the Anasazi people built a kiva, a sacred underground chamber in which the men could worship.

buckskin, most preferred cool and comfortable cotton clothing in the desert heat. A man's costume usually consisted of a kilt or full-length cotton pants, a loose cotton shirt, and buckskin moccasins, while a woman wore a belted knee-length cotton dress tied at one shoulder, and moccasins. She might also wear buckskin leggings to protect herself while gathering food from the prickly plants of the desert. Priests sometimes wore more elaborate ritual clothing, such as feather headdresses, specially patterned kilts and staffs, and fox skins. Women's hairstyles, particularly among such tribes as the Hopi, were often elaborate; one popular style, worn by a woman of marriageable age in which her hair was coiled up above her ears over a wooden framework, was known as the Squash Blossom. Like the Navajo, the Pueblo tribes were expert silversmiths.

Pottery is perhaps the best known of the Pueblo crafts. The women were the master potters of the Hopi, Zuni, and other Pueblos, and still create exquisite ware of local clays, intricately painted with geometric or representational designs as their ancestors have done for thousands of years.

Basketweaving was another ancient art; skilled weavers created everything from serving trays to cradle board frameworks for babies to containers for holding cornmeal. Cornmeal was produced on stone metates, or grinding boards.

Wood was used for the roof beams of Pueblo houses and their connecting ladders, for the hoes needed to cultivate the fields and, like the Navajo, for fire-starting friction drills and hand drills for making jewelry.

A metate, together with its grinding stone, is used for grinding corn.

Two Navajo women demonstrate the ancient, and still practiced, form of grinding corn using a grinding stone and a stone board known as a metate.

In the extreme south, the Papago and Pima hardly needed elaborate clothing. Women wore knee-length buckskin or cotton skirts. The Pima tribes cultivated the cotton and traded it with the Papago. Men wore breechcloths of buckskin or cotton. People generally went barefoot unless they were travelling a great distance, in which case they used simple sandals woven from twine. In the winter, men and women greased their upper bodies against the cold. Both men and women were proud of their long hair, which was considered a mark of beauty, and wore long, elaborate earrings of turquoise or other stones. They often painted their bodies; women, in particular, preferred attractive designs of butterflies or birds, and tattooed their chins for additional beauty.

The Papago and Pima tribes depended on cord made from the mescal plant for everything from rope to hold their homes together to baskets and carrying bags. A nomadic people in a hot climate hardly wanted to carry about heavy pottery, and a basket could be used for anything from food storage to (after it had been turned upside down) a drum. Cord-making was considered a man's work, but basketweaving and crocheting was a woman's job. Like the other Southwest tribes, the Papago and

The Chiracahua Apache created elaborate ornamentation for their coats with paint, fringes, and hair.

Two Apache babies look perfectly at ease in the cradle boards that hold them securely and shield their eyes from the sun.

The Spaniards brought sheep to the Southwest and the Navajo and other Pueblo peoples soon became skilled herders. Here, a Navajo woman shears precious wool from a sheep.

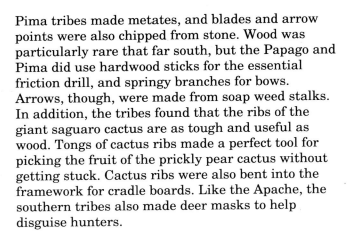

An Apache bride wears a long, elaborately fringed and beaded gown and several necklaces of shell and beads.

A Hopi basket weaver practices her craft in 1900. To her left sit several completed baskets woven of colored reeds.

Pima tribes made metates, and blades and arrow points were also chipped from stone. Wood was particularly rare that far south, but the Papago and Pima did use hardwood sticks for the essential friction drill, and springy branches for bows. Arrows, though, were made from soap weed stalks. In addition, the tribes found that the ribs of the giant saguaro cactus are as tough and useful as wood. Tongs of cactus ribs made a perfect tool for picking the fruit of the prickly pear cactus without getting stuck. Cactus ribs were also bent into the framework for cradle boards. Like the Apache, the southern tribes also made deer masks to help disguise hunters.

FOOD

When the Navajo first came into the Southwest, they were strictly nomadic hunters, dependant on whatever game they could kill or snare, and raiding the settled Pueblos. But when the Spaniards entered the region in the sixteenth century, the Navajo diet, along with that unsettled way of life, changed. Pueblo refugees taught them how to grow their own corn. And sheep stolen from the Spaniards began a long and successful tradition of sheep herding—carried out on horses also stolen from the Spaniards—that provided the Navajo with a steady diet of meat, supplemented by hunting, and a source of wool.

The Apache, unlike the Navajo—although they, too, raided the Spaniards freely—never took up sheep herding, depending instead upon what their men could take in the hunt, from deer and antelope to the smaller animals that even boys could catch. They also ate what women could gather from desert plants.

Women weave the famous Navajo rugs and blankets from some of their sheep's wool.

beans. Wild foods such as milkweed, watercress, and sagebrush were gathered by the women. Deer, gathered in drives, added welcome meat and provided valuable deerskin, and once the crops were grown well enough not to need as much attention, men could also hunt the smaller desert animals, such as the jackrabbit. Hunting and killing weren't undertaken lightly; the hunting party first made prayer offerings and smoked a sacred pipe to sanctify what they must do.

Even though the Papago and Pima lands don't look as though they could support human life, there is food to be had. The fruit of almost every cactus is edible, from the prickly pear, which needs only to have its thorns scraped away, to the cholla, which must be baked for a full day. The saguaro fruit could be eaten straight from the cactus, or turned into a sweet jam and drink. The saguaro seeds could even be ground into flour. There are also desert roots to eat, and the flowering stalks of the yucca. If the women should happen to gather more fruit than the tribe could eat right away, they dried it in the sun to preserve it, and sometimes buried the leftovers in caches for retrieval in the winter. The tribes also did plant some crops: corn, beans, and squash. The Pima, who lived closer to a constant source of water, had a larger harvest and depended less on the desert's uncertain bounty. It was the man's job to tend the fields.

Winter was the hunting season, when men went up into the mountains for deer drives. Everyone, men, women, and children, hunted the other desert animals, rabbits, ground squirrels, mice and rats, quail and doves. As a treat, the Papago and Pima tribes made a form of chewing gum out of the juice of the milkweed vine.

THE HORSE

Brought to the Southwest by the Spaniards in the sixteenth century, wild herds in the region meant little to the settled tribes of the Pueblos or to the southern semi-nomads like the Papago. However, the horse changed the Navajo way of life. A region with little water and sparse vegetation, sheep need vast areas in which to graze. With the new mobility their new mounts gave them, the Navajo could become successful sheep herders.

Chief Whitecloud from the Santa Clara Pueblo reservation plays a ceremonial drum in front of an ancient cliff dwelling in Manitou Spring, Colorado.

Life for the Pueblo peoples, as for farmers everywhere, revolved around the harvest. A vital part of the Pueblo diet was corn, which could be eaten fresh or ground into cornmeal. Among tribes such as the Hopi, cornmeal was the prime ingredient of *piki,* a thin bread which was a staple in the Hopi menu. It could be eaten plain, or as an accompaniment to stews. Such a stew often included vegetables grown by the tribe such as squash and

They could easily allow those sheep the room they needed, and were able to keep up with them. It meant, though, that as the various tribes followed their herds in the never-ending search for grass and water, the Navajo grew more and more widely dispersed over Arizona and New Mexico.

The impact on the Apache tribes wasn't quite so dramatic, but the horse also changed their lives. Until those first horses entered their region, the Apache relied on dogs as beasts of burden. Now, as had happened with the Plains tribes, they were suddenly mobile, able to travel swiftly over greater distances. Some of the tribes, like the Lipan Apache, who lived closer to the Great Plains, even became buffalo hunters.

And, as had happened with the Plains tribes, the horse meant one other change: it made raiding and warfare much simpler.

WAR

Although the Navajo and Apache tribes had a warrior tradition, and boys were trained as warriors as well as hunters or herders, outright warfare among the Southwestern tribes was a very rare thing. Raids for horses and other prizes were much more common among the Apache and Navajo tribes. The main point of an Apache raid, in fact—aside from stealing horses—was to totally avoid encountering the enemy; rites performed before a raid to ensure its success included rituals to help keep the raiders hidden. Unlike the Plains tribes, the Apache formed no warrior societies. Nor were they interested in taking scalps, possibly because of a taboo against touching the dead.

The Pueblo tribes, being farmers, were primarily involved with their crops, though they could and did fight fiercely when necessary. One of those occasions was when the Spaniards tried to conquer them. While some of the tribes were decimated, others, like the Hopi, impregnable in their adobe fortresses as knights in a medieval castle, held off the Spaniards so successfully that by 1680, the year of the Pueblo Revolt, they had driven the invaders away forever; the Hopi so totally shut out any Spanish influence that they refused to become Christianized, and practice their own faith to this day.

Geronimo, or Goyathlay in Apache, a famous war chief of the Apaches, kneels with his rifle in 1887. A year earlier, Geronimo surrendered to invading whites in the Arizona Territory.

The Papago and Pima tribes were, like the Pueblo peoples, more interested in protecting their crops than in fighting. But when they were raided by the Apaches, they retaliated. After rituals led by their tribal war leader, the "bitter man," they would march against the enemy, carrying bows and stone-tipped arrows, war clubs, and small leather shields. The Pima would attack in force, while the Papago preferred quick attacks made by only a few warriors. As soon as one of those warriors killed a man, he was believed to be engulfed by the magic power of death, and had to withdraw from battle to be purified. The Papago did take scalps, which were brought back to the women, who danced and sang songs of ritual triumph.

Apache Chief and Three Warriors, *by George Catlin, c. 1855/1869; National Gallery of Art, Washington; Paul Mellon Collection. This group portrait of an Apache chief and three warriors, provides an invaluable picture of Apache clothing and hairstyles of the mid-nineteenth century.*

DAILY LIFE

As a pregnant Navajo woman went into labor, she knew she was sheltered by the Blessing Way song, a chant retelling how the Holy People showed them how to live in harmony with the land. Her friends untied their hair to help "untie" the baby, and even the family horses and sheep might be released to further simplify the birth. Once the baby was born, it was anointed with sacred corn pollen and fed some of the pollen as well. A baby's first laugh was considered an occasion to celebrate.

Once a child had reached the age of seven, he or she was formally welcomed into the tribe by the Yeibichai ceremony, a short initiation rite which introduced the child to the Holy People of Navajo belief. The arrival of puberty was also the time for ceremony, particularly for a girl, whose new womanhood was celebrated by friends and family in a four-day rite known as Kinalda, at the end of which she was considered an adult, ready to marry. Among the Navajo, marriage within one's own clan was unthinkable, but there were few other problems for a young woman of marriageable age. She might meet many potential suitors at the tribal ceremonials and dances, and if a young man and woman fell in love, and if their families agreed, he would give her parents a suitable gift of horses, and build a hogan for himself and his new wife within her family's grouping.

Although the lines are beginning to break down nowadays, there used to be a strong sense among the Navajo of what was man's work and what could only be done by women. It was the men who built hogans and fences, who took care of the horses and herded the sheep, and the women who kept their homes, did the cooking, and farmed the crops, though a man might help his wife if she was ill or injured. It was also the women who did the weaving, but the men who dressed skins and worked with silver.

In their earliest days, Apache children were instructed in the proper ways of the tribe by their maternal grandmothers. A girl child was considered more valuable than a boy as the reproductive future of her people, but all children were welcome. As befitted a warrior people, boys and girls received the same physical training on foot and horseback; a child must be able to reach safety quickly in an attack, or defend him or herself if necessary.

As with the Navajo, the Apache celebrated when a girl reached puberty. She would be sponsored by an honorable woman of a different clan and dressed to represent one of the most powerful Apache religious figures, White Shell Woman. In a four-day ceremony of dances and chants, the girl would be symbolically invested with the gifts and abilities of womanhood. At the end of it, she could marry.

Like the Navajo, a boy and girl had some say in their decision to wed, although it was considered polite for their relatives to make the actual arrangements, culminating in the formal gift of horses by the boy to the girl's parents. As with the Navajo, the marriage was made formal by the boy

For all his obvious youth, this Apache boy sits as proudly as any adult warrior, showing off the patterns painted on his face and legs.

A Taos Pueblo man dresses in elaborate headdress and face paint for his tribe's Belt Dance.

Bert Cooley, a Pima farmer, sits in front of his home on the Gila River Reservation in Arizona. The well-known Pima cotton is one of the main crops grown by his tribe.

building a house for himself and his new wife in her family's house-cluster. Polygyny, the marriage of more than one wife, was sometimes practiced among the Apache, but it was rare. Since a man had to live with his wife's family, that meant keeping two separate households, a very expensive proposition. Divorce was possible for either side among the Apache, for such understandable reasons as cruelty, adultery, or incompatibility.

As with other tribes, the Apache divided labor between men's work and women's work, but the lines weren't always absolute. The women usually gathered wild plants and seeds, but men joined in the harvesting of agave crowns. Men were the prime hunters of the tribe, but women often participated in rabbit and antelope hunts. Women tanned hides for the family's clothing, but it was perfectly acceptable for men to help and mend their own clothing. Both men and women made their own tools. Only men were usually trained as warriors, but women often accompanied their husbands on raids. And some women, such as the famous Lozen, who fought beside Geronimo, became warriors in their own right.

Among the Pueblo peoples, a pregnant woman was careful to prepare herself and her baby well in advance by praying daily, keeping her hair and clothing free of knots and avoiding such taboos as looking at a snake, which might twist the child within her. When the time came for the birth, she would be surrounded by women from her clan, led by her mother, who would help her and pray with her. As with the Apache, a girl baby was particularly welcomed as part of the tribe's future. The father of the baby, meanwhile, lived apart from the family house for a ritual amount of time; he wouldn't even see his child until the naming ceremony, twenty days after the birth, when the baby was presented to the rising sun. A symbolic path of cornmeal sprinkled by the father set the baby correctly on the Road of Life.

As with the Navajo and Apache, a girl's puberty rites lasted for several days, and ended with her emergence from the darkened room in which she'd spent the time in ritual with her hair now in the squash blossom style that marked her as a young woman of marriageable age. The puberty rites for boys among the Pueblo tribes were more strenuous, involving tests of strength and bravery for the fledgling men and pitting them in a ritual battle against adults. When the mock battle ended in victory for the youngsters, they could proudly proclaim themselves adults, and would be allowed

Many Native American tribes loved games of chance. Here, four Paiute men enjoy a gambling session in Nevada.

into the men's kiva, the sacred pit-house forbidden to women.

Young people of tribes such as the Hopi were permitted, even expected, to experiment with *dumaiyas,* or love-trysts. The only real taboo was that one couldn't love a member of the same clan. Once a boy and girl had decided to wed, the girl went to live in the boy's home for three days, demonstrating her household skills to his mother. Meanwhile, a mock battle took place outside between the boy's female relatives on his father's and mother's side, involving much good-natured taunting of the boy and girl. When the three days were up, the young couple prayed to the rising sun

Children, of course, have their own special games. This group of Paiute children in Arizona play a variation on Tag known as Wolf and Deer.

Papago girls of southern Arizona play a form of hockey known as toku.

together and became husband and wife in the eyes of the tribe. They then went to live with the bride's family. Should a marriage not work out, either partner could initiate divorce.

Among the Pueblo tribes, the all-important job of farming was divided into work for men and work for women. The women were guardians of the seed; they inherited valuable seeds from their mothers, and selected the seed to be used for the next season's crop. The home was their domain; a woman owned her house and everything belonging to it, though she was forbidden the world of the kiva. Men did the actual farming, depending on the uncertain desert rainfall and seepage from the mesas on which the Pueblos sat to water their crops.

Unlike the Navajo, weaving was considered man's work among such Pueblo tribes as the Hopi. The man gathered and carded the cotton, then spun it into thread, although his wife would be the one to dye the thread with bright colors derived from local plants. Pottery making, though, and the making of woven baskets, was strictly the province of women, who were also responsible for preparing the family food and clothing.

When a Papago or Pima woman became pregnant, she and her husband obeyed a variety of taboos; he was even forbidden to hunt, for he must not risk taking life. The woman gave birth in a special house away from the home, to protect the rest of the family from the dangerous magic believed to surround something as miraculous as childbirth. After a month, the new parents were purified by the tribe's shaman, who gave the baby its name. Such true names held power, too, and were used only sparingly; nicknames were safer.

A growing child learned the proper ways of tribal life from his or her grandparents, and began doing everyday chores at an early age, though of course there was time for play, too. When a boy was old enough, he was expected to run till he was exhausted, then pray for a spirit animal to come to him as a guardian. Girls weren't expected to have such spirit-visions, but when a girl reached puberty, she gained such magic that she must be purified for the safety of those around her. Isolated for four days with an older woman for a teacher, she learned the ways of womanhood. After the four days of seclusion were over, her new status as an

Zuni Pueblos have been baking bread in hornos like this one for countless number of generations. They are considered by many to be master bakers.

adult was celebrated in a festival that might last for an entire month.

Young people of the Papago and Pima tribes had little say about their marriage arrangements, which were made by their parents. There was almost no ceremony; the new groom lived with his wife and her family for four days, after which they moved in permanently with his family. Divorce was possible; the woman would simply return to her own family.

Among the Papago and Pima, the men did the hunting and tended the family crops, and the women gathered plants and seeds, cooked, and made her family's clothing. Men did the weaving for the tribe and made the mescal string used in nets and baskets, though women did the actual basket making. Nowadays, the culture lines aren't quite so firm. Though Papago women do still gather some of the old foodstuffs, such as the fruit of the prickly pear and saguaro, the Papago have taken to raising cattle as their main industry.

A Cry Shed—carrying the prayers and tears of the tribe—was burned as part of the Hualapai Memorial Pow Wow held in Peach Springs, Arizona.

Hopi women dance in a ceremony in 1879 at Oraibi, Arizona.

The people of the Chaco culture belonged to a New Mexican branch of the Anasazi. Chaco Canyon, built in the ninth century A.D., is the largest prehistoric Southwestern pueblo. Seen here are the ruins of Pueblo Bonito, the largest Great House in the canyon.

RELIGION

The Navajo believe that the Holy People, supernatural beings of great power, have set down for them the proper path to walk to keep them in harmony with this world and that of the supernatural forces. As their daily rituals show, religion and life's chores weren't separated. To help them keep to the path, there were songs for every aspect of life, protective songs like the Evil Way chant warded off evil, ceremonial songs such as the Life Way chant healed the sick, some songs even celebrated the first laughter of a new baby. Spirit had dark sides, too, in the Navajo supernatural world. The *chinde,* malevolent ghosts, wait to destroy those who stray from the path, and witches, those people who have chosen to work evil, bring sickness and even death upon the unwary. Shamans counteract their evil, exorcising harm with elaborate ceremonies that include the famous Navajo sand paintings, sacred designs which are destroyed at the completion of the healing ritual.

The Apache feared the dangers of witchcraft, too. Disease was believed to be the result of a sorcerer's attack; such sorcery could be worked by magically shooting bits of bone or hair from a corpse into a living victim. Curing involved a shaman, who worked his or her magic to locate and remove the witch-arrow. If a shaman weren't doing his job, he could be blamed for such an event and called a sorcerer himself. But sickness or ill luck could also be brought about by chance; crossing the path of some animals such as the snake and the coyote could bring sickness or bad luck to the tribe.

Misfortune also could result from failing to properly respect the supernatural forces that watch over the Apache people. The Apache believe in many supernatural forces and in a supreme deity, Usen, Giver of Life. The Apache appeal to the spirit world for help, and celebrate it with ceremonies that involve masked dancers who impersonate these forces.

Pueblo life centered on the Kachinas, powerful supernatural beings who protect and bring prosperity to those who honored the old ways, and continue to be of vital importance to such tribes as the Hopi and Zuni today. For half the year, the Kachinas live in their spirit-forms in their own lands. But from the time of the winter solstice until the midsummer Niman Kachina festival, they live in the mortal Earth world, dwelling within human bodies, bringing vital gifts such as rain. Pueblos honored the Kachina spirits with Kachina dolls, treasured by children, and ceremonies in which masked dancers impersonate—or embody—the Kachinas. Everyone participated in the ceremonies.

Creating sand paintings is part of Navajo religious and healing ritual. When the ritual is over, the "painting" formed from carefully placed grains of colored sand is destroyed. This particular painting is called **Whirling Logs.**

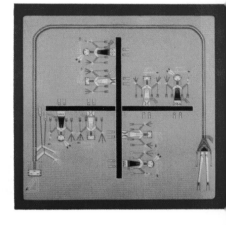

Early Picture Makers, *by Eanger Irving Couse, ca. 1925, oil on canvas, photographed by James Milmoe.*
Two small boys learn how to carve a petroglyph, or picture, into the side of a cliff in the Southwest. Native American petroglyphs can still be seen in such southwestern states as Arizona and New Mexico. (This image has been cropped.)

The Hopi use feathers in their religious ceremonies to bless objects or help them ask for divine assistance. A prayer feather has been placed on this metate, or grinding stone, to ask a blessing upon it.

135

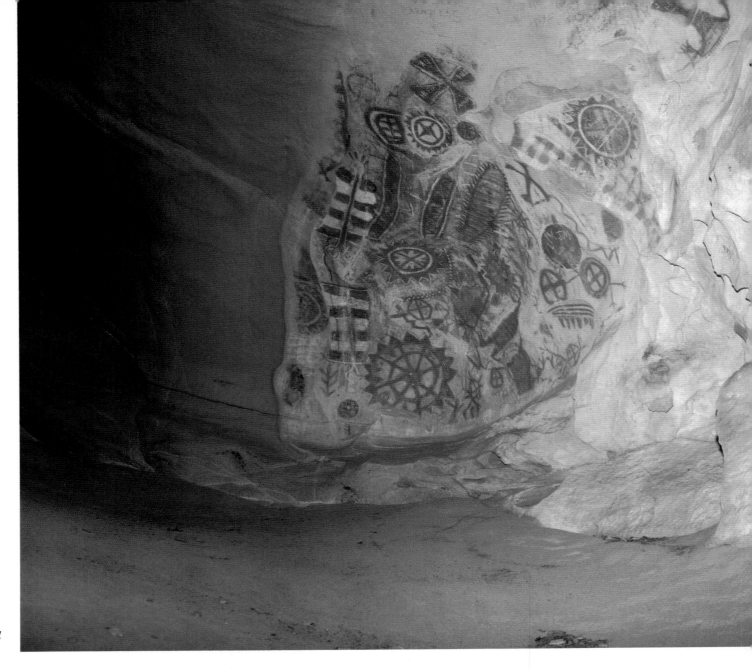

For millennia Native Americans have created cave paintings, called pictographs or pictoglyphs, leaving a record of their culture.

The Papago and Pima tribes believed that the world was created by the primal powers, Earthmaker and Itoy, with the help of Coyote. Itoy, Elder Brother to the Papago and Pima people, brought them forth from the lands underground, showed them how to live in peace with the world, that taught them the songs and ceremonies that would bring down the life-giving rain, or attract the deer, or make crops flourish. Though many of the tribes are Christian now, many others still sing the old songs and continue the traditional ceremonies.

By practicing traditional ceremonies, native americans keep their spiritual heritage alive.

DRIVEN TO THE RESERVATION

The first Europeans to enter the Southwest were, of course, the Spaniards, who drove the Pueblo peoples up onto their defensible mesas, where most of them remain today, many following the old ways. In some ways, Navajo and Apache life changed for good with the early invasion, providing them (against the Spaniards' wishes) with horses and, in the case of the Navajo, sheep and a profitable new business. Later, the invasion of other Europeans and Americans pushed them onto even smaller reservations. In 1846, the United States took possession of New Mexico and Arizona, building

Navajos captive.

Though it was an expensive victory for the United States, which now promised to care for the Navajo, they signed a treaty in 1868, giving them a 3.5 million acre reservation in northeastern Arizona and northwestern New Mexico. Though they returned to their homeland, it was devastated by the years of war. Later, the government broke its promise when building the Santa Fe Railroad in the 1880s. Even so, the Navajos have survived as a people and continue to travel along the path first set out for them by the Holy People.

During the nineteenth century and into the twentieth, the Papago and Pima tribes escaped the bloodiest battles between the other tribes and the United States. Their land was considered too barren for heavy white settlement. Today, modern Phoenix encroaches on Pima lands. Though far from wealthy, the Pimas raise a fine strain of cotton, which bears their name and brings money into the tribe. The Papago have become cattlemen, though because of the harshness of their desert land, they are among the poorest of the Native American tribes.

As with the Navajos, the warrior Apaches fought back against the United States Army in a protracted series of battles that produced such leaders as the famous Chiracahua Apache, Cochise. The

The Navajo, who learned agriculture from the settled Pueblo tribes, were farmers as well as hunters and sheepherders. Here a hogan near Holbrook, Arizona, overlooks rows of growing corn.

The Zuni painted colorful pictoglyphs on this rock near Gallup, New Mexico.

heavily armed garrisons on Navajo soil to oversee a never-ending stream of California-bound gold seekers who helped themselves to Navajo game.

The Navajo fought back in a series of bloody raids against the invaders and the United States Army. These battles on the government frontier continued through the years of the Civil War until, in 1862, it seemed as though the Navajo would be completely destroyed. Under the command of Colonel Christopher "Kit" Carson a combination of superior arms, a scorched-earth policy, and psychological warfare defeated the Navajo and ate at their culture. At the end of the struggle, United States forces held 8,000

Deer dancers of the Yaqui tribe of southern Arizona wear elaborate deer-head headdresses in their ceremonies.

138

Apache also lost to superior weaponry. In 1873, Apache bands were forced onto the San Carlos Reservation in Arizona. Although the war leader known as Geronimo continued to fight back until 1886, the old days of the warrior were numbered.

Today, the majority of Apaches live on adjoining reservations, San Carlos and Fort Apache, where they have become accomplished cattlemen. The Fort Apache Reservation, home to the White Mountain Apaches, also supports a thriving lumber industry, which in 1965 provided the White House Christmas tree. Like the Navajo, many of the Apache people today proudly keep alive the memories and time-honored ways of their ancestors.

Hopi Kachina figurines come in many forms. These dolls are known as mudhead or Kooyemsi.

These Hopi Kachina dolls, often given to Hopi children, represent the powerful Kachina Spirits of the Hopi faith.

With eagle masks on their heads, dancers prepare to perform at the San Juan Pueblo in New Mexico.

Contemporary Kiowa artist Steve Mopope portrays two Kiowa men dancing the sacred Eagle Dance in this watercolor. Sacred to many of the Native American tribes, eagles are believed to carry messages to and from the gods.

A Zuni drummer, dressed for a tribal celebration, chants as he drums, and wears impressive turquoise jewelry.

INDEX BY PAGE

Page Number	Photographer
4	National Museums of Canada
6-7	Slocomb/Chris Roberts Represents
8	National Archives
9 (left)	Cradoc Bagshaw
9 (right)	National Museums of Canada neg.# 91177
10	John Running
11 (bottom)	S. Leatherwood/PhotoEdit
11 (right)	National Museums of Canada neg.# 49489
12	Stephen Trimble
13 (bottom)	Mark Gibson
13 (top)	National Museums of Canada neg.# J-2434
14 (left)	National Museums of Canada neg.# 60610
14 (right)	Mark Gibson
15	Museum of the American Indian
16	Jerry Sinkovec
17 (top)	Rob Stapleton/M.L.Dembinsky Jr, Photo Assocs
17 (bottom)	National Museums of Canada neg.# J-3410
18 (top)	Gary Milburn/Tom Stack & Assocs
18 (bottom)	Gary Milburn/Tom Stack & Assocs
19	Slocomb/Chris Roberts Represents
20	Slocomb/Chris Roberts Represents
21	Cradoc Bagshaw
22	National Museums of Canada neg.# 255
23 (left)	Mark Newman/Tom Stack & Assocs
23 (right)	National Archives
24-25	K. Blackbird/Chris Roberts Represents
26	National Archives
27	Stephen Trimble
28	Eduardo Fuss
29	Rob Stapleton/M.L.Dembinsky Jr, Photo Assocs
30-31	Stephen Trimble
31 (top)	National Archives
31 (middle)	National Archives
31 (bottom)	National Archives
32 (left)	Jerry Sinkovec
32-33	Rob Stapleton/M.L.Dembinsky Jr, Photo Assocs
34-35	George Robbins
35 (right)	National Archives
36 (top)	National Archives
36 (middle)	National Archives
36 (left)	National Archives
36 (right)	National Museums of Canada neg.# 73457
37	Architect of the Capitol
38-39	Chris Roberts
39 (right)	National Archives
40 (top)	National Archives
40 (middle)	National Archives
40 (bottom)	W. Perry Conway/Tom Stack & Assocs
41 (left)	J. Wylder/Travel Montana
41 (right)	National Archives
42-43	1961.135 Amon Carter Museum, Fort Worth
43 (top)	1961.143 Amon Carter Museum, Fort Worth
43 (bottom)	National Archives
44 (left)	William Wilson
44 (top)	Museum of the American Indian
44 (right)	National Archives
45 (left)	Chris Roberts
45 (right)	Museum of the American Indian
46 (left)	Museum of the American Indian
46-47	Chris Roberts
47 (right)	Museum of the American Indian
48 (top)	Museum of the American Indian
48 (middle)	National Museums of Canada neg.# 74882
48 (bottom)	Museum of the American Indian
48-49	Stephen Trimble
50 (top)	National Archives
50 (bottom)	National Archives
51	Architect of the Capitol
52	Courtesy of The Rockwell Museum, Corning, NY
53	1961.147 Amon Carter Museum, Fort Worth
54	Courtesy of The Rockwell Museum, Corning, NY
55 (top)	National Museums of Canada neg.# 73458
55 (bottom)	Courtesy of The Rockwell Museum, Corning, NY
56	National Archives
57 (left)	Courtesy of The Rockwell Museum, Corning, NY
57 (right)	National Archives
58	National Gallery of Art
59 (top)	National Archives
59 (bottom)	National Archives
60 (top)	National Archives
60 (bottom)	Architect of the Capitol
61	National Gallery of Art
62 (top)	John Running
62 (bottom)	National Archives
63 (top)	National Archives
63 (bottom)	National Archives
64-65	Stephen Trimble
66	National Archives
67	Robert C. Dawson
68	Nevada Historical Society
69 (left)	Jerry Sinkovec
69 (top)	Museum of the American Indian
69 (bottom)	Museum of the American Indian
70	National Museums of Canada neg.# 20830
71 (left)	John Running
71 (right)	National Archives
72 (left)	Nevada Historical Society
72 (right)	Rob Stapleton/M.L.Dembinsky Jr, Photo Assocs
73 (top)	National Archives
73 (bottom)	National Archives
74	National Archives
75	Bob Pool/Tom Stack & Assocs
76-77	Architect of the Capitol
78	National Museums of Canada neg.# 594
79 (top)	National Museums of Canada neg.# 76024
79 (bottom)	Museum of the American Indian
80 (top)	John Running
80 (left)	National Museums of Canada neg.# 83930
80 (right)	National Museums of Canada neg.# J-2436
81	William B. Folsom
82 (left)	National Museums of Canada neg.# J-3243
82 (right)	William B. Folsom
83 (top)	National Museums of Canada neg.# 73464
83 (bottom)	National Museums of Canada neg.# J-2437
84 (left)	Rae Russell/International Stock Photo
84 (right)	Museum of the American Indian
85	National Gallery of Art
86 (left)	National Museums of Canada neg.# 72218
86 (right)	National Museums of Canada neg.# 73999
87 (top)	M. Timothy O'Keefe/Tom Stack & Assocs
87 (bottom)	National Archives
88	William B. Folsom
89	Florida Tourism
90	William H. Allen
90-91	John Running
92 (left)	Mark Gibson
93	Bob Daemmrich/Image Works
94 (left)	Museum of the American Indian
94-95	Mark Gibson
96	Florida Tourism
97 (bottom)	National Archives

97 (right)	National Archives
98 (left)	National Archives
98-99	John Running
100-101	Stephen Trimble
102-103	Stephen Trimble
104	Eduardo Fuss
105 (left)	John Running
105 (right)	National Archives
106	Stephen Trimble
107	Eduardo Fuss
108-109	Jerry Sinkovec
110	Stephen Trimble
111 (top)	Jerry Pavia
111 (bottom)	National Archives
112 (top)	National Archives
112 (bottom)	Stephen Trimble
113	Stephen Trimble
114 (left)	National Archives
114 (bottom)	National Archives
115	Tom Till/International Stock Photo
116-117	John Running
117	Mark Gibson
118 (left)	Museum of the American Indian
118-119	John Running
119 (right)	National Archives
120 (left)	National Archives
120 (bottom)	National Archives
120-121	John Running
122	Mark Gibson
123 (top)	National Archives
123 (bottom)	National Gallery of Art
124	Stephen Trimble
125 (left)	Bob Winsett/Tom Stack & Assocs
125 (right)	National Archives
126-127	Stephen Trimble
128 (left)	National Archives
128-129	John Cancalosi/Tom Stack & Assocs
129 (right)	National Archives
130	Stephen Trimble
131	Stephen Trimble
132 (left)	National Archives
132-133	P. Barry Levy/Profiles West
134	Courtesy of The Rockwell Museum, Corning, NY
135 (bottom)	Stephen Trimble
135 (right)	Museum of the American Indian
136-137	Mark Gibson
137 (top)	National Archives
137 (bottom)	Jerry Sinkovec
138	Stephen Trimble
139 (top)	Stephen Trimble
139 (bottom)	Bob Smallman/International Stock Photo
140	Eduardo Fuss
141 (left)	Eduardo Fuss
141 (right)	Museum of the American Indian

INDEX BY PHOTOGRAPHER

Photographer	Page Number
William H. Allen	90
Amon Carter Museum, Fort Worth	42-43, 43 (top), 53
Architect of the Capitol	37, 51, 60 (bottom), 76-77
Cradoc Bagshaw	9 (left), 21
K. Blackbird/Chris Roberts Represents	24-25
John Cancalosi/Tom Stack & Assocs	128-129
W. Perry Conway/Tom Stack & Assocs	40 (bottom)
Robert C. Dawson	67
Bob Daemmrich/Image Works	93
William B. Folsom	81, 82 (right), 88
Florida Tourism	89, 96
Eduardo Fuss (left)	28, 104, 107, 140, 141
Mark Gibson	13 (bottom), 14 (right), 92 (left), 94-95, 117, 122, 136-137
S. Leatherwood/PhotoEdit	11 (bottom)
P. Barry Levy/Profiles West	132-133
Gary Milburn/Tom Stack & Assocs	18 (top), 18 (bottom)
Museum of the American Indian	15, 44 (top), 45 (right), 46 (left), 47 (right), 48 (top), 48 (bottom), 69 (top), 69 (bottom), 79 (bottom), 84 (right), 94 (left), 118 (left), 135 (right), 141 (right)
National Archives	8, 23 (right), 26, 3 (top), 31 (middle), 31 (bottom), 35 (right), 36 (top), 36 (middle), 36 (left), 39 (right), 40 (top), 40 (middle), 41 (right), 43 (bottom), 44 (right), 50 (top), 50 (bottom), 56, 57 (right), 59 (top), 59 (bottom), 60 (top), 62 (bottom), 63 (top), 63 (bottom), 66, 71 (right), 73 (top), 73 (bottom), 74, 87, 97 (bottom), 97 (right), 98 (left), 105 (right), 111 (bottom), 112 (top), 114 (left), 114 (bottom), 119 (right), 120 (left), 120 (bottom), 123 (top), 125 (right), 128 (left), 129 (right), 132 (left), 137 (top)
National Gallery of Art; Washington; Paul Mellon Collection 1965	58, 61, 85, 123 (bottom)
National Museums of Canada, Canadian Museum of Civilization	4, 9 (right), 11 (right), 13 (top), 14 (left), 17 (bottom), 22, 36 (right), 48 (middle), 55 (top), 70, 78, 79 (top), 80 (left), 80 (right), 82 (left), 83 (top), 83 (bottom), 86 (left), 86 (right)
Nevada Historical Society	68, 72 (left)
Mark Newman/Tom Stack & Assocs	23 (left)
M. Timothy O'Keefe/Tom Stack & Assocs	87 (top)
Jerry Pavia	111 (top)
Bob Pool/Tom Stack & Assocs	75
Chris Roberts	38-39, 45 (left), 46-47
The Rockwell Museum, Corning, NY	52, 54, 55 (bottom), 57 (left), 134
George Robbins	34-35
John Running	10, 62 (top), 71 (left), 80 (top), 90-91, 98-99, 105 (top), 116-117, 118-119, 120-121
Rae Russell/International Stock Photo	84 (left)
Jerry Sinkovec	16, 32 (left), 68 (left), 108-109, 137 (bottom)
Bob Smallman/International Stock Photo	139 (bottom)
Rob Stapleton/M.L.Dembinsky Jr, Photo Assocs	17 (top), 29, 32-33, 72 (right)
Slocomb/Chris Roberts Represents	6-7, 19, 20
Tom Till/International Stock Photo	115
Stephen Trimble	12, 27, 30-31, 48-49, 64-65, 100-101, 102-103, 106, 110, 112 (bottom), 113, 124, 126-127, 130, 131, 135 (bottom), 138, 139 (top)
William Wilson	44
Bob Winsett/Tom Stack & Assocs	125 (left)
J. Wylder/Travel Montana	41 (left)

Note: The "Architect of the Capitol" paintings belong to the United States Capitol Art Collection

Special thanks to Walter James, Jr. and Anthony Saenz who have helped make this project possible.

APPENDIX I

NATIVE AMERICAN ORGANIZATIONS

American Indian Culture Research Center
Box 98
Blue Cloud Abbey
Marvin, South Dakota 57251

American Indian Law Association
960 Walhonding Avenue
Logan, Ohio 43138

Bureau of Indian Affairs
Department of the Interior
1951 Constitution Avenue NW
Washington, DC 20245

Council for Native American Indian Progress
280 Broadway
New York, New York 10007

Institute for the Study of American Culture (ISAC)
(Before Columbus)
New York Chapter
280 Broadway, Room 316
New York, New York 10007

Institute of American Indian Arts
Alexis Hall
St. Michaels Drive
College of Santa Fe Campus
Santa Fe, New Mexico 87501

National Native American Chamber of Commerce
225 Valencia Street
San Francisco, California 94103

North American Indian Museums Association
c/o Seneca Iroquois National Museum
Allegany Indian Reservation
P.O. Box 442
Salamanca, New York 14779

APPENDIX II

FURTHER READING

Billard, Jules B., Editor. *The World of the American Indian.* Washington, D.C.: National Geographic Society, 1989.

Driver, Harold E. *Indians of North America* (2nd edition). Chicago: University of Chicago Press, 1969.

Erdoes, Richard and Alfonso Ortiz. *American Indian Myths and Legends.* New York: Pantheon Books, 1984.

Gordon, Cyrus H. *Before Columbus: Links between the Old World and Ancient America.* New York: Crown Publishers, Inc., 1971.

Jenness, Diamond. *The Indians of Canada.* Ottawa: National Museum of Canada Bulletin 65, 1934.

Josephy, Alvin M., Jr., Editor. *The American Heritage Book of Indians.* New York: American Heritage Publishing Company, 1961.

Mahan, Joseph B., Jr. *The Secret: America in World History Before Columbus.* Columbus, Georgia: J.B. Mahan, 1983.

Maxwell, James A., Editor. *America's Fascinating Indian Heritage.* New York: Reader's Digest Association, Inc., 1978.

Ney, Marian Wallace. *Indian America: A Geography of North American Indians.* Cherokee, North Carolina: Cherokee Publications, 1986.

Waldeman, Carl. *Atlas of the North American Indian.* New York: Facts on File Publications, 1985.

Wolfson, Evelyn. *From Abenaki to Zuni: A Dictionary of Native American Tribes.* New York: Walker and Company, 1988.